Blessings:

To order additional copies, please contact us.
BookSurge, LLC
www.booksurge.com
1-866-308-6235
orders@booksurge.com

Blessings:
Adventures of a Madcap Christian Scientist

Karen Molenaar Terrell

2005

Blessings:

For Elsie, Junie, and Mozzy – three sisters from a noble generation – with much gratitude for the precious gift they have given me.

"And God saw everything that he had made, and, behold, it was very good."
Genesis I: 31

INTRODUCTION

***

"Happiness is spiritual, born of Truth and Love.
It is unselfish; therefore it cannot exist alone,
but requires all mankind to share it."
From *Science and Health with Key to the Scriptures*
by Mary Baker Eddy

***

Years ago an old boyfriend said to me, "I can't see that Christian Science has made you any better than anyone else."

"I know!" I said, nodding my head in complete and happy agreement, "But can you imagine what I'd be like without it?!"

He raised his eyebrows and laughed. What could he say? He was looking at a self-centered, moralistic, stubborn idealist who saw everything in terms of black and white. But I could have been worse. I believe without Christian Science I would have been worse.

Let's get one thing clear from the start: I am not the best example of a Christian Scientist. I'm not as disciplined as I could be. I have fears and worries and doubts. I'm a little neurotic. I am the Lucy Ricardo of Christian Scientists.

I should probably put in a disclaimer here, too — the views expressed in these pages are not necessarily the views shared by other Christian Scientists. Christian Scientists are really a pretty diverse group of people — there are Democrat Christian Scientists and Republican Christian Scientists, "Green," and "Red," and "Blue" Christian Scientists, and Christian Scientists with no political affiliations at all. Frankly, I like that about us. We keep each other on our toes.

I should also tell you that this book is not an authorized piece of Christian Science literature. If you want to actually study Christian Science you should probably read the textbook for this way of life, *Science and Health with Key to the Scriptures* by Mary Baker Eddy.

My purpose for writing this epistle is really two-fold (I don't think I've ever used the word "two-fold" in my life, and using it now is making me feel sort of professorial. I like the feeling.):

First-foldly, to introduce you to one Christian Scientist so that if you ever hear someone talking fearfully and ignorantly (feargnorantly?) about Christian Scientists you'll be in a position to say, "I have a friend who's a Christian Scientist, and, although it's true she's a bit of a nut, she's also…" and you can go on and talk about how your friend has used her study of Christian Science to try to make the world a happier place.

Second-foldly, I feel the need to acknowledge God's blessings in my life. I don't want to be like those nine lepers in the Bible who couldn't take the time to thank Jesus for healing them. I want to be like that one leper who "fell down on his face at his feet" before Jesus and gave him thanks (Luke 17). Through my study of Christian Science I've witnessed some incredible proofs of our Father-Mother God's love for Her creation in my life. God has filled my life with infinite blessings and it's time for me to acknowledge these blessings to others.

BLESSINGS:

COUNTING MY BLESSINGS

✻✻✻

"Are we really grateful for the good already received?
Then we shall avail ourselves of the blessings we have,
and thus be fitted to receive more."
From *Science and Health with Key to the Scriptures*
by Mary Baker Eddy

✻✻✻

Okay, so in this dream I'm about forty, right? Unmarried, child-less, substitute teaching, and living with my parents, God bless their hearts. For extra money, my folks are suggesting I sell lemonade and bottled water to the bird-watchers who are touring their acreage (don't ask, it's a dream, work with me here).

I'm feeling trapped, claustrophobic, desperate for escape. I can't believe I've made it to forty and have nothing to show for it. Am I going to be living with my parents forever? Will I never find love or a career or have a family of my own? And how am I supposed to get our visiting bird-watchers to spend money on my lemonade?

I have no idea how long this dream actually lasted, but when I was finally able to shake myself awake, I breathed a huge sigh of relief and, like George Bailey in *It's a Wonderful Life*, began to count my blessings. Okay, so maybe the house my husband, Scott, and I owned was a hundred years old and needed a little work. And alright, maybe I hadn't become the famous singer-writer-actor-ice-skater-world-traveling-world-admired sophisticate I'd once fantasized about becoming.

Things could be worse. I could be peddling lemonade in my parents' back forty to a merry band of traveling ornithologists.

THE TIES THAT BIND

✱✱✱

"Divine Love always has met and always will meet every human need."
From *Science and Health with Key to the Scriptures*
by Mary Baker Eddy

✱✱✱

Actually, my blessings began before I was even conceived.

In 1953 my dad was on a mountaineering expedition on K-2, the second highest mountain in the world, and considered by many climbers the hardest in the world to climb. A member of his climbing team fell, ropes got tangled, and five men found themselves careening down a steep and icy slope, out of control, with no hope of being able to stop themselves.

Fortunately for them, Pete Schoening was a member of their team. Pete kept the five falling men from certain doom with a belay that has come to be known as "The Belay" in the annals of mountain-climbing history. Because of Pete's courage, quick-thinking, and strength, my dad and his comrades survived that fall and made it back to civilization where they took up their lives and proceeded to reproduce.

I've often thought of the children born to these men at least nine months after this expedition as the "Children of the Belay" and, although I've never met all the other spawn of these adventurers, I feel a certain connection to them.

One of the Children of the Belay is Pete's daughter, Kim. Besides the fact that our dads were both on the expedition to K-2, Kim and I have many things in common. We both were raised in the mountains of the Pacific Northwest by our dads, raised in Christian Science by our moms, and married men from the east coast. When Kim married she moved to upstate New York with her husband, Rich. When my husband's parents retired they moved to a place about forty miles away from Kim and Rich, and so our trips to the east coast have often included visits with them.

Another thing Scott and I had in common with Rich and Kim—although we never discussed this with them—was the desire to have children.

Almost eight years after we were married Scott and I finally became parents with the birth of our son, Andrew. As anyone knows who's ever longed for years to have a child and finally been blest with one, it seems a miraculous, wondrous thing to finally be holding your own child in your arms.

And you know how when something good happens to you, you want it to happen to your friends, too?

So every morning when I woke up I would talk with God about Kim and Rich, and how it seemed such a pure and right and natural thing for them to have a child. I knew they would both be great parents.

Two months after my son was born a former Sunday School student of mine asked to speak with me after church. Coincidentally, my former pupil was named Kim. Although no one would have been able to guess by looking at her, Kim was seven months pregnant. With tears in her eyes she told me that she loved the baby she was carrying, but she'd come to feel that the baby didn't belong to her. She asked me to pray with her to know that the baby would be brought to his rightful home.

So—picture this if you will—I woke up every morning praying for Kim Schoening and her husband to have a child, and in the next breath I was praying for Sunday School Kim's baby to be brought to his right home.

I'm embarrassed to admit that it took a week for me to see the obvious.

Sunday School Kim went through an hour of labor and after two pushes (no, I'm not kidding) gave birth to a beautiful baby boy. She told me it was as if she'd never been touched by the pregnancy or the birth. Because the baby was born early, Kim agreed to nurse him for a few weeks. But even as she nursed him, she knew he didn't belong to her. When it came time to put him in the arms of Kim Schoening she was able to do so with nothing but joy.

Kim Schoening's family gave a baby shower for the new baby. When I visited them later I asked Rich to show me the gifts they'd received at the shower. Rich held up a little shirt in awe and said, "We got this." Then he carefully laid it down and picked up a little sweater, "And this," he said, handing me the sweater. He continued, reverently showing me each pint-sized t-shirt and each pair of booties and overalls. There was something very touching about seeing this grown, bearded man tenderly handling each of his son's gifts.

It's been almost thirteen years now since the adoption. Today Sunday School Kim is happily married with two healthy young sons of her own. Kim Schoening and Rich were blest with the birth of a second son two years after they adopted their eldest. And Scott and I were blest with our second son not long after they had theirs.

Pete Schoening passed away last year. I miss his energy, his positive approach to life. And I will always be grateful to him for keeping my dad alive on K-2. I once pointed out to Pete that if he hadn't saved my dad's life on K-2 he wouldn't have been blest with his grandson. The idea made him smile. Pete's wife says, "These are the ties that bind." I like that thought—that we're all bound together with love. And how awesome that the good Kim's father did for my father came back to him thirty-eight years later in the form of a grandson. You just never know how the good you do today will affect your future, do you?

THE STATE RELIGION

***

"Verily, verily, I say unto you, He that believeth on me, the works that I do shall he do also; and greater works than these shall he do; because I go unto my Father."
John 14:12

"To ignore God as of little use in sickness is a mistake. Instead of thrusting Him aside in times of bodily trouble, and waiting for the hour of strength in which to acknowledge Him, we should learn that He can do all things for us in sickness as in health."
From *Science and Health with Key to the Scriptures*
by Mary Baker Eddy

***

Medical Science has become our State Religion. I've been asked if I believe in doctors in the same hushed tones people use to ask one another if they believe in God. But, to my way of thinking, asking me if I believe in doctors is akin to asking me if I believe in plumbers or teachers or secretaries. Doctoring is a profession, it's not a Divine Truth. And, as in any profession, some doctors are wonderful, dedicated human beings and some are not.

For me the question isn't really whether or not I believe in doctors, the question is how much do I believe in God? I was raised to turn immediately to God for every challenge I faced, and Christian healing was just a natural, every day part of my life. Instead of turning to a little inanimate pill for healing, or visiting a doctor – I learned to go right to the top, to the Head Guy. I suppose this might seem wacky to some people. Heck, it might seem wacky to me, too, if I'd been raised differently. But there it is. Any honest medical doctor will tell you that medical science is not an exact science. Its theories about cause and effect, diagnosis and prescription and cure, are forever changing. Sometimes, too, the medicine that is given to cure one ailment will create side effects that are as bad as the original problem.

In Christian Science, the physical healing is the side effect of a better understanding of God. Taking a pill isn't going to make you a better person — you're not going to become more moral or spiritually-minded or have a greater understanding of God through medical science. But getting a better understanding of God is what healing in Christian Science is all about. Every time an individual experiences healing through God's power it brings him closer to understanding the might and allness of God.

There are a lot of misunderstandings about Christian Science. Probably a few of these misunderstandings about my way of life are created by some of my fellow Christian Scientists.

For instance, a couple of years ago my mother-in-law, a kind and God-loving Methodist, finally admitted to me that she'd been a little concerned when her son had told her he was marrying a Christian Scientist. Apparently her step-grandmother had been a student of Christian Science and she had been one of the not-so-nice variety—a money-grubbing, rigid old lady without an ounce of compassion in her cranky old soul, whose method for dealing with sickness was to pretty much ignore it and hope it would go away.

My own mother, on the other hand, was one of the nicest kinds of Christian Scientists. She was a pure expression of Love and always tackled life's challenges head on with the healing power of the Christ which she learned through her study of Christian Science. Sharing her understanding of Christian Science is the greatest gift she gave to her children. I still recall with great gratitude the nights Mom, or "Mozzy" as we called her, would come to me as I lay in bed with legs aching from playing outside all day. Mozzy would sit on the side of my bed and gently rub my legs and sing hymns from the *Christian Science Hymnal*. I remember her singing these words in particular (attributed to Frances A. Fox): "In Thee, O Spirit true and tender, I find my life as God's own child; Within Thy light of glorious splendor I lose the earth-clouds drear and wild. In Thee I have no pain or sorrow/ No anxious thought, no load of care. Thou art the same today, tomorrow; Thy love and truth are everywhere." I remember the feeling of being surrounded in a warm, light-filled bubble of Love, God, and the pain in my legs melting away.

***

The first big physical healing I ever witnessed was the healing of my younger brother, Peter. Pete had been in a great deal of pain and my dad, who wasn't a Christian Scientist, wanted to take him to the doctor. My mom always respected my dad's wishes regarding medical treatment, and joined Dad in taking my brother to the local physician. The doctor told my parents that Peter was "a very sick boy" and had mastoiditis. He told them that Peter would need to have surgery, might lose his hearing, and was in danger of dying.

I didn't know any of this at the time. I just knew my little brother was screaming and crying and hurting.

As my dad mixed up medicine for Pete over the kitchen sink, my mom asked if she could call a Christian Science practitioner for help. Dad put the medicine aside and gave mom 24 hours to heal Peter with Christian Science. Mom called the practitioner and told her about Pete's problem, asking the practitioner for her prayerful support.

This is the part that I remember very clearly: I was lying in bed that night, listening to my brother crying in the next room. I could hear Mom singing hymns to him, comforting him, telling him about his identity as God's perfect reflection. Then – in an instant! – the screaming turned into snoring. My mom called out, crying in joy, "He's healed! He's healed!"

And he was, too!

That kind of experience is hard to forget, discount, or ignore. It has stayed with me for forty years and is still as clear and dear to me as the night it happened.

My brother was brought back to the doctor who verified the healing. My dad, who was a very practical man in matters of money, realized that the Christian Science practitioner was a lot cheaper than a doctor and more effective, and pretty much entrusted his children to Christian Science after that.

***

The first successful Christian Science treatment I remember giving myself involved a wart. The wart was on one of my fingers, and I remember playing with it, digging little grooves in it with my fingernail – it was like a toy, I guess. Then one day a woman noticed the wart and I heard her tell my mom that there was medication that could get rid of it. That's when I decided I better heal this thing with Christian Science. I can't remember now how I actually prayed about it, but I remember that within a couple of days I looked down at my finger and the wart was gone!

Another childhood memory I have of a physical healing involved a broken arm. I was big into high-jumping when I was in fifth grade and my dad had made a little high jump for me in the backyard. In those days high-jumpers didn't land on a cushiony mattress, they landed on a pile of sawdust, and so Dad had thrown down a sort of ritual scattering of bark chips for me to land on. It was the end of the day, the sun was setting, and I decided I had it in me to do one more jump. I jumped. I landed horizontal on the ground—the bar between my arm and my body—and felt something snap in my arm. I looked at my arm and the wrist was in the shape of a "V." "Well, this doesn't look right," I thought to myself, pushing up on the bottom of the "V" to make it go back up. "Mom?" I called, "This doesn't look right."

Mom took one look and began praying. Dad took one look and loaded us all up in the Rambler to go to the hospital. So here's my dad – world-famous mountain-climber, member of the local Mountain Rescue volunteers, World War II veteran – freaking out. "Hold her arm! Hold her arm! She's going to be crippled for life!" he ranted. My mom calmly sang hymns and reassured me everything would be fine.

When we got to the hospital I told the doctor I didn't want any pain medication. Mom held my hand while he set my arm. When he was finished, Mom said, "Honey, I think your father needs me more than you do right now," and let go of my hand. I looked down on the floor next to the examining table. There was my dad, spread-eagled on the floor, unconscious.

The doctor told my parents that I'd probably need to come back in a day or two to have the arm reset and the cast adjusted, telling them that my arm would probably swell in the next 24 hours. The next day he called to find out how I was doing (he was one of those wonderful, dedicated type of doctors). My mom told him I was outside playing baseball, and asked him if he wanted her to call me in so he could talk to me. He laughed and said that if I was playing baseball I was probably doing alright.

My arm didn't swell up or have to be reset and when I returned for a check-up four weeks later, the doctor said my arm was completely healed and took the cast off two weeks early.

***

The final childhood healing I remember happened several years after the broken arm.

When I was fourteen or so, I went on a back-packing trip along the ocean with some other Christian Science high-schoolers.

The first evening, as we were setting up camp, I sat on a nest of yellowjackets. When I first felt the stinging, I thought I'd gotten some nettles up my pants (this was when wide bell-bottom jeans were "in"). But when I felt the "nettles" moving around and crawling up my legs, I quickly realized I was dealing with something else entirely.

I jumped up and began trying to shake the wasps out of my pants. My fellow hikers thought I was doing a crazy Karen-dance and rooted me on with applause and laughter until they realized what was actually happening. Then someone quickly set up a tent for me, I took my jeans off, and the tent filled up with yellowjackets as they escaped from my pant's legs. I had stings all up and down my legs.

There was a Christian Science practitioner on the back-packing trip, and she immediately began praying for me.

I remember that at one point, as everyone was sitting around the campfire that night, I began to have the weird sensation that I was drifting away. My hearing became dulled. It was like voices were coming to me from a great distance. This scared me a bit, and I quietly told the practitioner that it felt like I was "moving away from everybody." She continued to pray with me.

A passage from *Science and Health* by Mary Baker Eddy came to me, "…all of God's creatures are useful, harmless, and indestructible…" I knew that the yellowjackets were included in this statement, too. God couldn't create anything that would harm another of Her creations.

***

Well, I survived. But I remember being scared of wasps and bees for awhile after that. What finally cured me of my fear was a bumblebee that had gotten trapped in my bedroom. He was buzzing back and forth across the window, desperate to escape outdoors. My heart went out to him. I got a glass and a piece of paper, put the glass over him, slid the paper underneath him, and took him outside. As it says in the *Scriptures*, "Perfect love casteth out fear…" I haven't been afraid of bees since.

My God is Love. My God is good.

PEAK MOMENTS

***

"I will lift up mine eyes unto the hills,
from whence cometh my help."
Psalms 121:1
"Spiritually interpreted, rocks and mountains
stand for solid and grand ideas."
From *Science and Health with Key to the Scriptures*
by Mary Baker Eddy

***

Some of the most amazing blessings I've experienced in my life
I've experienced in the mountains.

I climbed my first real mountain, Oregon's Mount Hood, at 15.
To tell you the truth, I don't remember a whole lot about that experience, except that my face sunburned into a crispy, tomato-red mask.

But the next mountain I climbed was Mount Rainier, and I remember *that* climb very well....

***

I lived and worked in Paradise in Mount Rainier National Park
for two summers between my college years. They were some of the
best summers of my life. Imagine living in a place where world-class
waterfalls, thousands of acres of alpine wildflowers, and a sleeping
volcano are part of your backyard, where you're surrounded by other
healthy, happy young college kids who have the same love for the
mountains that you do (Ah! The romance!), and where you have the
opportunity to hike some of the finest trails in the world every day
after work.

After the tourists had gone home for the day, my friends and I
would often sit on "The Wall" (a rock wall that bordered the Para-

dise parking lot). It was a peaceful, quiet, thought-expansive time of the day. As we watched the sun set in pink and gold behind the mountain, my friends and I would wax philosophical about life and love, and hopes and dreams.

It was while my friend, Perky, and I were sitting on The Wall one evening that it came to me it was time to climb Mount Rainier. "Perky," I said, nodding to Rainier, "We are going to climb that mountain this summer."

Two weeks later my Dad, brother, Perky, and several other friends from Paradise found ourselves on the slopes of Rainier. Destination: The Top.

***

We woke up at Camp Muir, the base camp for this climb, at one in the morning to prepare for our climb to the summit. I remember how cold it was, fumbling with my crampon laces with numb fingers, feeling excited and nervous about the climb ahead. While we'd climbed up to Camp Muir we'd been in a thick fog and weren't sure we'd be able to do the climb. But once we'd reached Muir the clouds had thinned, and it looked like we'd be able to get to the summit, after all. (God has always blest me with good weather for my mountain-climbing adventures.)

As we started out, there were a golden half-moon and silver stars glittering in the night sky overhead, and soon, as we scrabbled and scraped our way across the gravelly scree slope in our crampons, the sky began to glow orangey-pink behind Little Tahoma. In those moments just before the sun appeared I felt pressed near to God's creation, wrapped up in the beauty of His expression.

I saw amazing things that day – things that you can't witness "down below." Above timberline, in the glaciers of a mountain, you enter another world. I saw deep blue crevasses with huge icicles hanging down into them, and "suncups" – fields of snow and ice that have evaporated without melting – forming shapes that look like little castles.

We reached the summit seven or eight hours after leaving Camp

Muir. There were no bands playing and no parades up there. There was no view, either — the clouds had moved in and encircled the summit. But we'd done it! We'd made it to the top! God had blest us all with strength and endurance for the climb. Once again, I realized the unlimited possibilities we each have as God's ideas.

***

About every ten years or so after the climb of Rainier I would get the insatiable urge to climb another big mountain — to get up in the rocks, snow, and ozone again. In my thirties I climbed Mount Baker with my dad, husband, and some teaching friends. And when I hit forty I decided it was time to climb Washington's second highest mountain, Mount Adams.

I should probably explain that, through all the previous climbs, I'd just followed my dad up to the summits and followed him down again. I'd never become very skilled with self-arrest, which is the technique a climber uses to stop himself should he be falling down a snow or ice slope. Nor had I developed any competence or confidence in glissading — which is a technique climbers use to shoosh themselves down a mountain, using their ice axes to steer (I'd had a harrowing experience glissading as a teenager and had suffered from a fear of it ever since).

Now Mount Adams is one of the few mountains in the Cascades on which you don't have to contend with any crevasses. Consequently, because climbers don't need to dodge crevasses when descending, there are these huge chutes going straight down the slopes that have been carved out by the successive derrieres of dozens of glissaders. All a climber needs to do is throw herself into one of these chutes and push off to travel down the mountain for several hundred feet. Everyone in my climbing party planned to use these chutes to get off the mountain once we reached the summit. I knew that I'd have to face one of my great fears on this mountain.

My dad was 79 that summer and, though he started the climb with us, at about 10,000 feet he began to feel he was holding us back (which actually wasn't true — I was enjoying his steady pace) and turned back for base camp. I can't describe the thoughts that raced through my head as I watched Dad head back. I'd never before climbed a major mountain without him! It felt weird to be heading for the summit sans Pop.

This is not Christianly Scientific for me to say, but I have to admit that one of my chief motivators for continuing to go up was the fear of going down. But eventually, of course, we reached the summit and, figuring there was no point in prolonging the inevitable, I suggested to my comrades that we should start down as soon as we took some quick victory pictures.

I reached the first chute and took a breath. "Fear not, for I am with thee. Be not dismayed, for I am thy God," came the words from *Scripture*. Bravely, I sat down and pushed off. Nothing happened. My wool pants stuck me to the snow like Velcro. This was an anticlimactic moment. I began to row myself down the chute with my ice axe.

I'd gotten about half-way down the chute when I heard a "whoosh" behind me. My husband, Scott, in his slick windpants, was barreling down the chute toward me, picking up speed as he came. I began to row frantically.

I am blest to be married to a man who is calm, cool, level-headed. Unlike me, he didn't panic as he descended upon me. Without missing a beat, or slackening his pace, he opened his legs out to either side of me and sort of wedged me in between them as we went careening down the chute together.

I gripped onto his boots with white-knuckled hands — in the same way a person riding a roller coaster might grip the bar holding her to her seat — and prayed.

This was a particularly long chute with lots of curves and twists. It made for a wild ride. Simultaneously screaming in terror and laughing in exhilaration, I hit the fluffy snow wall that marked the end of the chute, Scott tumbling into it after me.

We had survived.

Scott pulled me up, brushed the snow off me, and decided it might be wise to give me a quick refresher course on how to self-arrest and steer with my ice axe.

BLESSINGS:

Tentatively at first, and then with more confidence, I began to practice using my ice axe. Soon I was rushing happily from one chute to the next, looking forward to the ride, eager to practice what I was learning. In no time at all our little troop was nearing base camp.

As we got close to camp I saw the figure of Dad climbing up to meet us. When he reached us he hugged me and said, "I've never before had to be the one that waits at base camp." Shaking his head, he added, "I don't like the worry of it."

Wow! This had been a big day for Dad, too! Being the one who watches and waits had probably been harder on him that coming down Mount Adams had been for me.

Basking in our mutual admiration we made our way down to the camp together.

***

When my oldest son, Andrew, was four, Dad joined us for a hike up Pinnacle Peak. I had climbed Pinnacle Peak at the same age Andrew was now, and we were carrying on the tradition with him.

The hike up to the Pinnacle Saddle was uneventful and fun. Andrew's little legs were moving at a good clip and he showed no signs of being tired at all. I was enjoying being back in the mountains again, and loving the fact that I was with both my father and son on a trail that had happy memories for me.

Most people stop when they reach the Pinnacle Saddle, or go to the right and hike up to Plummer Peak. But we turned left at the Saddle, to scramble up the rocks to Pinnacle Peak. There is some danger there. The rocks are loose and a climber has to make sure he has a stable and secure handhold as he's climbing, and he must be alert to rocks falling from above.

Dad roped us up for the last pitch to the top and I was so proud of the way little Andrew went confidently moving up through the rocks, without any hesitation or fear. When we got to the top, Dad gave Andrew his own can of root beer – a special treat for him – and we celebrated Andrew's first rock climb. It was a glorious moment.

We again roped up for the descent, Dad belaying Andrew and

I from above as we made our way down. At some point Dad accidentally let loose a rock that went bouncing off the rock wall and smacked into Andrew's hand as he gripped onto a boulder. Andrew's face crumpled and his eyes teared up. He was trying very hard not to cry—he didn't want his grandpa to feel bad about accidentally hurting him—but when I got close to him he whispered to me what had just happened to his hand.

"Shepherd, show me how to go o'er the hillside steep," I sang to him, sharing with him the words by Mary Baker Eddy to a hymn from the *Christian Science Hymnal* that he was familiar with from Sunday School. Andrew quietly sang the hymn with me and we prayed together to know his identity as God's image and likeness, and to know that none of us is ever separated for a moment from God's love and care. By the time Dad joined us the tears had dried up on Andrew's face, and he was fine.

Riding home in the car from our adventure – Andrew, Dad, and Mom (who'd waited for us down below) nestled into the Subaru with me – I was filled with such gratitude to God for giving us this wonderful day together.

***

Alexander, my youngest son, had a shining moment in the mountains several years later.

Scott, the boys, Mom, Dad, and I had all decided we'd hike up Mt. Pilchuck. The hike up to the lookout tower on Pilchuck can be challenging. Mom and Dad (who, that summer, were 75 and 85 respectively) told us early on in the hike to just go ahead of them, and they'd go at their own pace and see how far they could get. We heeded their words and took off up the trail.

It was a hot day and once we came out of the trees for the last pitch to the top we were exposed fully to the sun. I wasn't doing well with the heat and the glare that was coming off the boulders and it seemed to take every last bit of energy for me to get to the top of Pilchuck that day. The view from the top is spectacular. Scott, the boys, and I spent about twenty minutes up there just looking around and resting, before heading down.

We'd gotten about half a mile from the top when Mom and Dad emerged from around a corner. I couldn't believe they'd managed to make it that far (but probably shouldn't have been surprised given the kind of people my parents are). I was very proud of them. While I'd been flitting around, trying to dodge the sun, my parents had patiently trudged along, step by step, and were now almost to the top!

At this point Andrew and I were wiped out, both struggling with a belief of heat stroke probably. We couldn't summon the energy to go back up to the top with Mom and Dad and crawled into the shade of a hemlock tree. Alexander looked at both of us incredulously! It was beyond belief to him that we'd expect Grandpa Dee and Grandmozzy to climb up to that lookout by themselves! I have to admit to feeling a little guilty when Alexander looked at me like that—but not guilty enough to move out of the shade. (As I said in the "Introduction," I'm not always the best example of a Christian Scientist. Case in point.)

Alexander, who had grumbled about how tired he was all the way up to the lookout – and understandably, he was only eight years old at the time and his legs were half as long as anybody else's—suddenly was filled with renewed energy. He wanted to be with his grandparents when they reached the top. Scott elected to go back up, also, and the four of them set out for the lookout tower.

I was very proud of Xander that day. I heard him laughing and giggling as he skipped along behind his grandparents, so happy to be with them. Love was leading him on. As Mary Baker Eddy writes in *Science and Health*, "Love illumines, designates, and leads the way."

As for Andrew and me? As we waited for everyone to rejoin us, we had a grand time sipping lemonade and eating trail mix and talking about what wonderful people we have in our family.

FROM CURSING TO BLESSING

✷✷✷

"Every trial of our faith in God makes us stronger."
From *Science and Health with Key to the Scriptures*
by Mary Baker Eddy

✷✷✷

Okay, so there was this woman I knew. She was not a girly girl. She'd been raised with brothers, a mother who had no interest in accessories or luxury, and a mountain man for a father. Cosmetics and frou-frou clothes were not a part of her life as she grew up. Instead of a purse, she had her faithful hiking backpack. Instead of high heels, she had her tennis shoes and boots.

She was what you would call a late bloomer in the romance department. She was awkward around men and very self-conscious about any feminine wiles that might inadvertently peek out of her persona. Feminine wiles were not highly valued in her family and it was a little embarrassing to have any. There were young men who were attracted to her, but in her teens and early twenties she was mostly oblivious to their attraction or scared of it. There were young men to whom *she* was attracted, too, of course — but she mostly enjoyed fantasizing about them from afar, rather than having an actual relationship with any of them, and on those rare occasions when she took it in her head to try to flirt with one of them she had no idea how to go about it.

There came a day, though, when for the first time our heroine took interest in a male thigh. It was in the mountains of Colorado and the man who came with the thigh was young, confident, and easy to flirt with. Our heroine was twenty-two and for the first time realized that there might be more to find in the mountains than a good hike.

Not long after her epiphany about male thighs and other things male, a Dutch jazz musician entered her sphere. Now here was someone expert with the ways of romance. They spent almost a year together, culminating in a trip to The Netherlands to spend time with his family.

The Netherlands was the home of our heroine's ancestors, and she felt a certain kinship with the people there. She loved the land—the tangy, saltwater smell of it, the wide open flatness and the canals, the black and white cows, the white lace curtains, the brick streets, the oldness and history. But, alas, there were no mountains to climb there. And, further alas, the Dutch jazz musician became someone she didn't know when he stepped back onto his native soil.

In an autumnal Dutch wood on a sunny Dutch day, they both agreed that a certain kind of love and a certain kind of hate are very closely related and snipped the cords of their romance.

The relationship had to end. Our heroine knew that. But knowing it didn't seem to make it any easier. It felt like someone she loved had died. She came home from Europe with her tail between her legs, dark circles under her eyes, and weighing about the same as Tinkerbelle.

I think most people have experienced heartbreak at least once in their life. It's a part of growing-up really. Makes us more empathetic to the pain of others, makes us more compassionate, and that's a good thing—a blessing. And as Mary Baker Eddy writes in *Science and Health with Key to the Scriptures*, "Every trial of our faith in God makes us stronger."

***

It took our heroine a few months to recover and then she earnestly entered what she has come to call her "dating phase." She was meeting men everywhere—parking lots, the supermarket, the workplace, hiking, through friends. These men were talented, witty, and smart—a German physicist, a teacher cum comedy script writer, a sweetheart of a man who introduced her to cross-country skiing for the first time—and it was a heady thing for her to have them all show an interest in her.

BLESSINGS:

At first the dating phase was great fun. Because her life wasn't committed to one person she had the freedom to go and do what she wanted, meet and date all these interesting men, take road trips on impulse, head for the hills on a whim, with no one else's schedule to have to negotiate.

But about the time she turned twenty-six something began to change in her thought. Singlehood began to lose its charm and these men she'd been meeting all started to seem the same to her. Dating became a little monotonous. She felt unsatisfied with the lack of direction in her life. She was beginning to feel it was time to get serious about this relationship thing and stop dinking around.

In a moment of self honesty, she admitted to herself she'd been going out with the wrong kind of men for what she now needed and wanted in her life. Mary Baker Eddy writes in the chapter entitled "Marriage" in *Science and Health*: "Kindred tastes, motives, and aspirations are necessary to the formation of a happy and permanent companionship." And so our heroine made a list of qualities that she wanted to find in someone: She wanted to meet a man of compassion and integrity; If this man was going to be a part of her life he'd also need a sense of humor, believe me; And he'd have to love the mountains, of course; and she'd really like him to have some kind of a creative, stimulating occupation; And, as a last whimsical thing, she decided that he'd come from either California, Colorado, or Connecticut. She'd gone out with short men, tall men, blond, dark, wiry, and sturdy—and they'd all been attractive to her. But an image of The One came to mind: He'd be about six feet tall, lanky, have brown hair, and glasses.

***

In December of '82 a woman named Peggy, whom our heroine had met a couple of years before through the Dutch jazz musician, invited her to her wedding. To be honest, our heroine had no intention of going to this wedding, not wanting to mingle with all these people she'd met through the Dutchman. But on the eve of the wedding the woman who was scheduled to be the wedding singer got laryngitis and asked our heroine if she could take her place as the singer. She'd never sung at a wedding before, but asked herself, "How hard could it be?" and agreed to sing a song or two.

***

She spotted him as soon as she got there. The wedding was an informal affair held in a living room, and this man with a camera—the wedding photographer, she guessed—was weaving his way through the people who were seated and waiting for the wedding. Everywhere he stopped to chat, people would start chuckling. She surmised he must have a sense of humor. And he had a great smile—the full-faced, crinkly-eyed kind.

She found herself instantly attracted to him.

The wedding began, the ceremony proceeded, she sang her song (a little nervously), and kept her eyes on the man with the camera.

After the ceremony she, who had until now always been the pursued rather than the pursuer, walked up to him and introduced herself. He blinked behind his glasses, probably surprised at her directness, and grinned down at her. "Scott," he said, shaking her hand.

At the reception, held in a local community hall, they talked and got to know each other better. She asked him if he liked the mountains. He said yes. She asked him if he'd ever climbed any. Yes, he said, Mt. Baker. She mentally put a check by the "loves mountains" on the list of qualities she was looking for in a man. Their conversation continued. She learned he was a newspaper photographer and checked off the requirement for "stimulating, creative job." She saw how he opened the kitchen door to help an elderly woman with her hands full. "Compassionate" was checked off her list.

He asked her if he could fetch her something to drink. She told him she'd really just like some water. He nodded his head. "Wadduh, it is," he said.

"Wadduh?" she asked. "Are you from the east coast?"

"Connecticut," he answered, grinning.

***

BLESSINGS:

A year and a half later Scott got a call from Peggy. Our heroine answered the phone. She told Peggy that her husband wasn't home right then, but could she take a message? When she heard the caller's name she let her know her own. Peggy admitted she'd heard rumors that Scott and she had married. She was happy to have had a part in their meeting each other.

Scott and our heroine have been happily married for over twenty years now.

And our heroine realizes that she wouldn't have been blest with her love if she hadn't first met the jazz musician. From cursing to blessing. It's all connected.

THE HONEYMOON

***

"In heavenly love abiding,
No change my heart shall fear;
And safe is such confiding,
For nothing changes here.
The storm may roar without me,
My heart may low be laid;
But God is round about me,
And can I be dismayed?"
From the *Christian Science Hymnal*, words by Anna L. Waring

***

It had been the perfect day for a spring wedding—sunny and warm, with the perfume of daffodils, plum blossoms, and freshly-mowed grass filling the air. We played volleyball in my parents' field – the groom's team won, but the score was close – and ate lemon wedding cake and deli-style sandwiches.

As we drove away in our official honeymoon car – my little white Toyota Corolla – Scott and I turned to wave good-bye to our friends and family and then faced forward to begin our new life together. We were off to a happy start. Our friends had decorated our car, declaring us to be "Just Married," I was holding a fragrant bridal bouquet and wearing a new wedding ring, and Scott had my crown of baby's breath wrapped jauntily around his head. Life was full of glorious possibilities.

***

Then suddenly—whack! A little bird ricocheted off the windshield and onto the road. Scott pulled the car over and we ran to help the bird. He was still alive. We squatted down next to him and it was then that we noticed what was happening under our car — a stream of oil was gushing out of it and onto the road. I scooped the bird into my hands and onto the side of the road, then we rushed back to the car and drove back to my parents' home.

Arriving back at their house was an anticlimactic moment.

There was obviously no way we were going to be able to take the Corolla any further, so we loaded everything into Scott's truck and decided that, at this point, we would just spend the night at his (now our) house in Seattle.

***

We had our wedding dinner at the Wendy's by the Seattle-Tacoma airport. Those of you with a sense of humor don't need me to say anything more about that. I expect those of you with no sense of humor stopped reading this book long ago.

But there is one really cool blessing that happened to us at Wendy's: We got married during the weekend for college basketball's Final Four, which was being held in Seattle that year, and there were about half a dozen African-American men ranging in height from 6'8" to 7'0" waiting in line with us to order burgers. Naturally, being the socially graceful person I am, I came right out and asked the question everybody else at Wendy's wanted to ask — "Hey! Are you guys basketball players?" They grinned down at me and admitted that they were, indeed, players from Georgetown come to claim National Collegiate victory. "Wow! Cool! Good luck with that!" I said, shaking their hands. And then, of course (being the socially graceful person I am), I had to tell them that my husband and I had just gotten married that day. They all congratulated us and wished us the best. I gathered my courage and asked, "Do you think we could get your autographs?"

They looked around stealthily, trying to see if their coach was near. "Well," one of them said, "We're not really suppose to give out autographs, but for you guys — seeing as how you just got married and everything — sure! We can do that for you!" And he signed our receipt and then passed it around for the others to sign. (I still have that receipt, by the way – signed by Billy Martin, Ralph Dalton, and Horace Broadmax – God bless them!)

That weekend the Georgetown team went on to win the National championship, Scott and I rooting for them all the way.

***

The next day Scott and I left on our honeymoon trip down to the Oregon coast, and I think I can safely say that no other couple on earth has ever had quite the same honeymoon experience.

The first day I developed a yeast infection like I had never before and have never since experienced. The second day I crushed my fingers in the truck door as, all excited, I leaped out of the vehicle to take in a spectacular view of the ocean. The third day I pinched a nerve in my back. By day four we decided it would be best to return to Seattle. No sooner had we gotten back than Scott's office called (hoping to find him home on the off-chance that he'd decided to end the honeymoon early) to ask him if he could come in to work. By that evening I was curled up in the fetal position on our bedroom floor, wondering if this is what my entire married life would be like – full of pain and suffering – and chanting, "I want a divorce. I want a divorce. I want a divorce." Scott opened the door, saw me rocking and moaning on the floor, and calmly asked, "What would you like for dinner tonight?"

This was exactly the right way for him to respond to me – no gnashing of teeth, no belittling and no sympathy, either – just, "What would you like for dinner tonight?"

That night Scott laid down the law. He said he couldn't stand to see me suffering like this and he was taking me to the doctor tomorrow. I knew I would not be going to the doctor the next day, but I also knew that this was the moment when I had to establish my new life on a foundation of Christian healing. Sometimes my prayers are rather intellectual exercises, sometimes my prayers are full of humor at the absurdity of material life, but this time my prayer was a heartfelt call to God. "You have never let me down, God, and I know you won't let me down now, either! I know you can heal me! I know you *will* heal me!"

All the pain went away in that instant. I told Scott, "I'm healed," and went to sleep.

***

A few years later Scott observed, "You know with other Christian churches when you get healed it's a really big deal – a miracle. With Christian Scientists it's just an every day thing." God bless that wonderful Methodist boy!

THE CHRISTMAS DOG

❋❋❋

"This is the doctrine of Christian Science: that divine Love cannot be deprived of its manifestation, or object; that joy cannot be turned into sorrow, for sorrow is not the master of joy; that good can never produce evil; that matter can never produce mind nor life result in death."

From *Science and Health with Key to the Scriptures* by Mary Baker Eddy

❋❋❋

Christmas Eve, 1988. I was in a funk. I couldn't see that I was making much progress in my life. My teaching career seemed to be frozen, and I was beginning to think my husband and I would never own our own home or have children. The world seemed a very bleak and unhappy place to me. No matter how many batches of fudge I whipped up or how many times I heard Bing Crosby sing "White Christmas," I couldn't seem to find the Christmas spirit.

I was washing the breakfast dishes, thinking my unhappy thoughts, when I heard gunshots coming from the pasture behind our house. I thought it was the neighbor boys shooting at the seagulls again and, all full of teacherly harrumph, decided to take it upon myself to go out and "have a word with them."

But after I'd marched outside I realized that it wasn't the neighbor boys at all. John, the dairy farmer who lived on the adjoining property, was walking away with a rifle, and an animal (a calf, I thought) was struggling to get up in the field behind our house. Every time it would push up on its legs it would immediately collapse back to the ground.

I wondered if maybe John had made a mistake and accidentally shot the animal, so I ran out to investigate and found that the animal was a dog. It had foam and blood around its muzzle. She was vulnerable and helpless—had just been shot, after all—but instead of lashing out at me or growling as I'd expect an injured animal to do, she was looking up at me with an expression of trust and seemed to be expecting me to take care of her.

"John!" I yelled, running after the farmer. He turned around, surprised to see me. "John, what happened?" I asked, pointing back towards the dog.

A look of remorse came into his eyes. "Oh, I'm sorry you saw that, Karen. The dog is a stray and it's been chasing my cows. I had to kill it."

"But John, it's not dead yet."

John looked back at the dog and grimaced. "Oh man," he said. "I'm really sorry. I'll go finish the job. Put it out of its misery."

By this time another dog had joined the dog that had been shot. It was running around its friend, barking encouragement, trying to get its buddy to rise up and escape. The sight of the one dog trying to help his comrade broke my heart. I made a quick decision. "Let me and my husband take care of it."

"Are you sure?"

I nodded and he agreed to let me do what I could for the animal.

Unbeknownst to me, as soon as I ran out of the house my husband, knowing that something was wrong, had gotten out his binoculars and was watching my progress in the field. He saw the look on my face as I ran back. By the time I reached our house he was ready to do whatever he needed to do to help me. I explained the situation to him, we put together a box full of towels, and he called the vet.

As we drove his truck around to where the dog lay in the field, I noticed that, while the dog's canine companion had finally left the scene (never to be seen again), John had gone to the dog and was kneeling down next to her. He was petting her, using soothing words to comfort her, and the dog was looking up at John with that look of trust she'd given me. John helped my husband load her in the back of the truck and we began our drive to the vet's.

BLESSINGS:

I rode in the back of the truck with the dog as my husband drove, and sang hymns to her. As I sang words from one of my favorite hymns (based on a hymn by John R. MacDuff) from the *Christian Science Hymnal*—"Everlasting arms of Love are beneathe, around, above"—the dog leaned against my shoulder and looked up at me with an expression of pure love in her blue eyes.

Once we reached the animal clinic, the veterinarian came out to take a look at her. After checking her over he told us that apparently a bullet had gone through her head, that he'd take care of her over the holiday weekend—keep her warm and hydrated—but that he wasn't going to give her any medical treatment. I got the distinct impression that he didn't think the dog was going to make it.

My husband and I went to my parents' home for the Christmas weekend, both of us praying that the dog would still be alive when we returned. For me, praying for her really meant trying to see the dog as God sees her. I tried to realize the wholeness and completeness of her as an expression of God, an idea of God. I reasoned that all the dog could experience was the goodness of God—all she could feel is what Love feels, all she could know is what Truth knows, all she could be is the perfect reflection of God. I tried to recognize the reality of these things for me, too, and for all of God's creation.

She made it through the weekend, but when we went to pick her up the vet told us that she wasn't "out of the woods, yet." He told us that if she couldn't eat, drink, or walk on her own in the next few days, we'd need to bring her back and he'd need to put her to sleep.

We brought her home and put her in a big box in our living room, with a bowl of water and soft dog food by her side. I continued to pray. In the middle of the night I got up and went out to where she lay in her box. Impulsively, I bent down and scooped some water from the dish into her mouth. She swallowed it, and then leaned over and drank a little from the bowl. I was elated! Inspired by her reaction to the water, I bent over and grabbed a glob of dog food and threw a little onto her tongue. She smacked her mouth together, swallowed the food, and leaned over to eat a bit more. Now I was beyond elated!

She'd accomplished two of the three requirements the vet had made for her!

The next day I took her out for a walk. She'd take a few steps and then lean against me. Then she'd take a few more steps and lean. But she was walking! We would not be taking her back to the veterinarian.

In the next two weeks her progress was amazing. By the end of that period she was not only walking, but running and jumping and chasing balls. Her appetite was healthy. She was having no problems drinking or eating.

But one of the most amazing parts of this whole Christmas blessing was the relationship that developed between this dog and the man who had shot her. They became good friends. The dog, in fact, became the neighborhood mascot. (And she never again chased anyone's cows.)

What the dog brought to me, who had, if you recall, been in a deep funk when she entered our lives, was a sense of the true spirit of Christmas—the Christly spirit of forgiveness, hope, faith, love. She brought me the recognition that nothing, absolutely nothing, is impossible to God.

We named our new dog Christmas because that is what she brought us that year.

Within a few years all those things that I had wondered if I would ever have as part of my life came to me—a teaching job, children, and a home of our own. It is my belief that our Christmas Dog prepared my heart to be ready for all of those things to enter my life.

FINDING HOME

***

"Pilgrim on earth, home and heaven are within thee,
Heir of the ages and child of the day.
Cared for, watched over, beloved and protected,
Walk thou with courage each step of the way."

***

These words, from one of my favorite hymns in the *Christian Science Hymnal,* are words that I have turned to often as my husband and I have sought to make manifest "home" in our lives.

We bought our first home about fourteen years ago. To the mortal eye, that house probably didn't look terribly grand. It was very small, with a postage stamp-sized yard and a kitchen badly in need of remodeling. But we loved that home. We painted, remodeled, reroofed, and planted a garden. We brought our first son home to that house and he took his first steps on the green shag carpet of the living room.

Not long after he was born, though, we realized we were going to need more space.

One day I was driving by a turn-of-the-century craftsman-style house that had always appealed to me and I noticed a "for sale" sign in front of it. On impulse, I called the number listed on the sign. The woman who answered the phone happened to be the same woman who had sold us our first house. I asked her if my husband and I could take a tour of the newly-vacant house. Within the hour we found ourselves walking through the front door.

As soon as I walked into that house I knew I was home. The linoleum on the floor was cracked, the kitchen needed work, the walls were badly in need of a paint job, but I didn't see any of that. I turned to my husband and said, "I love this house!"

I told the real estate agent that we hadn't even put our old house on the market yet, though. She said we could just trade it in to her real estate company and use it as down payment on this house. I'd never heard of such a thing before, but that's exactly what we did.

We spent seven wonderful years in that home, and our second son took his first steps in its backyard.

As the children got older, though, we began feeling that we'd like to build a home from scratch, so we began looking for property. But nothing seemed right for us: The water table was too high on this one; the slope too steep on that one; and a third property was too close to a busy road.

It was when I was beginning to feel the most frustrated about this search that a real estate agent said calmly to me, "Don't panic. When it's right it will happen." As a student of Christian Science, her words struck an immediate chord in me. Years before I'd heard a Christian Science lecturer say something very similar: "There is never too little, too much, too late, or too soon."

We decided to stop looking for property and concentrated our efforts on making our current home more comfortable.

About a year later a friend of mine suggested that we check out a house that a co-worker of hers was selling. We walked through it with the owners, but, although a lovely home, it just didn't feel like it was ours. As we were leaving my husband told the owners that what we were really looking for was property to build on. They told us their neighbor was thinking of selling the two acres next door. In my husband's words, it was a "prime piece of land" and we called on the owners to ask about it.

We felt an immediate kinship with these people. They said they'd sell us the two acres as well as the home they were living in and the half acre that came with it for a very reasonable price.

My husband explained to them that we'd need some time to get our house ready to put on the market, and they offered to fix the closing date as six months down the road!

When it came time to sell our house I remembered the real estate agent who'd once said, "When it's right it will happen" and asked her to help sell our house. The house was sold within two weeks. The transaction went so smoothly that even the real estate agent seemed to be in a state of shock. "I've never seen anything like this," she said.

"But you said when it was right it would happen," I reminded her.

"Yes, but I didn't mean like this!" was her response.

We moved into the house next to our property and began to build our home. I had moments of panic. Would we be able to sell the house we were living in before we had to start making payments on the house under construction? Would our next house be ready for us to move into before we had to move out of our old house?

But in my moments of panic I would turn to the teachings of our way-shower, Jesus Christ. Jesus said, "Seek ye first the kingdom of heaven and all these things shall be added unto you"—reminding me of what my priority should be—knowing and expressing God.

Again using the real estate agent that we'd used to sell our previous house, this house was sold within two weeks and the new owners agreed to a closing date three months in the future, giving time for our new home to be completed before we had to move out of our old one.

Another family in our neighborhood had been trying to sell their house for many months and called our real estate agent to find out how we had managed to sell our house so quickly. Our real estate agent told them my husband and I just seemed to do this kind of thing really well. The woman in the family then called me to ask for advice. Knowing this family was devoutly religious I felt very comfortable in speaking with her about the power of God. I told her what the real estate agent had told me—"When it's right it will happen"—and said I was convinced that God was watching over all of his children, that none of us is left out of his care, and none of us is separated from His love.

Soon they were able to sell their house and move to their new home in California.

Later, when talking with my real estate agent about how comforting her words, "When it's right it will happen," had been for me,

I learned her grandmother had been a Christian Science practitioner. Although the real estate agent was not a practicing Christian Scientist herself, I have to admit that the fact her grandmother had been one made me grin. It is, indeed, a small world.

I am convinced that, as that wonderful hymn says, "...home and heaven are within us." It has been such fun to see that sense of home made manifest in our lives and in the lives of others.

BLESSINGS:

BABY LOVE

***

"To attend properly the birth of the new child, or divine idea,
you should so detach mortal thought from its material conceptions,
that the birth will be natural and safe.
Though gathering new energy,
this idea cannot injure its useful surroundings
in the travail of spiritual birth.
A spiritual idea has not a single element of error,
and this truth removes properly whatever is offensive.
The new idea, conceived and born of Truth and Love,
is clad in white garments.
Its beginning will be meek, its growth sturdy
and its maturity undecaying."
From *Science and Health with Key to the Scriptures*
by Mary Baker Eddy

***

December 4, 1991
Childbirth class stinks!
The film we saw last night showed a woman who had to have a caesarean. The instructor called this film much more realistic than the first film where four women all had natural, normal birthing experiences. Obviously, my reality is different from our instructor's. If one woman on this planet has had a perfect, harmonious birthing experience than there is no reason for any other kind of birthing experience.

***

December 8, 1991
Karen: It's going to be a good baby.

Scott: It's gonna be a *great* baby!

Karen: Have you been talking to it?

Scott: Mentally, I think about it all the time.

Karen: What do you think about it?

Scott: I think about how amazing it is that we're going to have a baby. I think about how happy I am. (Scotty apparently puts his hand on my belly and feels the baby move while I'm sleeping. How cool! They have their own special time together!)

***

December 13, 1991

We have a son! He was born yesterday at 7:01 pm, weighing in at seven pounds, five ounces. His length was 19 and a half inches. He has nails and a little smattering of wavy, dark hair. He's beautiful.

He keeps getting carted in and out of our room for tests and so forth. Last time he was absconded, Scotty got really restless, pacing the room, "I want my son back!" he growled, and went in search of him.

***

December 15, 1991

When my belly started going down a few days ago I found myself beginning to miss it. I've gotten so use to lugging my little buddy around in there. Now I need to get use to lugging him around on the outside. My favorite time has been lying next to him in bed at night and watching him sleep — it's so cozy and warm, and it makes me feel secure to hear his soft breathing next to me.

***

December 23, 1991

Last night with Andrew tucked in beside me, I sang, "Sometimes in the morning when shadows are deep, I lie here beside you just watching you sleep, and sometimes I whisper what I'm thinking of — my cup runneth over with love." It was a precious moment — Andrew just lay there and sweetly watched me sing my tribute to him – he's still so innocent, can't tell me to stop singing, can't say, "Ick, Mom!"

**

January 3, 1992

Such pleasure to feel Andrew's warm little head nestled under my chin, to feel his little body next to me in bed. So wonderfully unnerving to open my eyes and find him studying my face, or to sing to him and watch him looking at my mouth, as if he's trying to imitate me. Incredible to hold him close to me at the doctor's office and see him calm down and stop crying because he's in my arms, trusting me.

**

January 11, 1992

There's something very poignant about seeing Andrew's little clothes laying around the house. He's real. A month ago he wasn't here, now his sweet presence fills our home.

**

February 7, 1992

On our walk to Jones Creek this morning the neighborhood malamute dog came out to greet Andrew and me, followed closely by her tiny puppy. This malamute has always avoided us before – but this time she seemed eager to come to us, and it was obvious she was proud to show off her puppy. She politely sniffed at Andrew as if to say, "You have a beautiful puppy, too!" and beamed at me when I held *her* baby. It was a cool moment – the two mothers showing off their pups.

**

March 3, 1992

I was reading a section of an Agatha Christie novel out loud to myself today while Andrew lay in my lap, nursing. After I was done speaking lines from the book, I looked down at Andrew and he was watching me, his mouth open, eyes latched onto mine, listening to me with intense focus. I started laughing, and he grinned and went back to nursing.

Cozy to nurse him in bed, with the rain tapping on the roof and windows outside.

***

March 16, 1992
Andrew's been flirting with me lately — as he's nursing he'll stop and look at me out of the corners of his eyes and grin. What a charmer!

***

April 12, 1992
Went for a walk with Christmas Dog while Scott watched Drew. When I came back Drew's whole face lit up and he smiled at me. I hope he'll always light up like that when he sees me. I know I make him happy right now — I'm part of his security and confidence in life — he trusts me. Please God, let me always be there when he needs me.

***

April 14 1992
Tonight while Drew took a break from nursing he looked up at me, grinned, and licked his top lip — it was so cute!

***

April 28, 1992
We're at the ocean. Got here Sunday afternoon. Went for a walk along the beach with Drew on Sunday, but he was asleep. He was asleep again yesterday when we took him for a second walk, but at the end of this walk we woke him up to dip his feet in the ocean and take a photo. As we started to head back to the motel I noticed that Drew was really focused on the ocean for the first time. So I brought him back down to the water's edge. He stared at the ocean then — eyes alert and moving back and forth, sucking on his lower lip. He wouldn't

take his eyes off of the water. Can you remember what it's like to see the ocean for the first time? The hugeness of it! The sound and smell? It's fun to watch Andrew tune in to it for the first time.

***

May 12, 1992

Now when I pick Andrew up and he's sleepy or hungry he'll wrap his arms around my neck and suck on my cheek.

Everyone is constantly telling me what a "beautiful" baby he is. When he was a newborn, people often told me that he looked complete and whole and real, not like a typical new baby. When he was four weeks old someone told me that Andrew looked like a real person, had a grown-up face, a real nose.

***

June 30, 1992

Andrew is not a little stranger any more. I know him now. His laugh, his grin. The way he looks when he's sleepy, the way he turns his head, and reaches for my face, and sings — all these are familiar to me now.

He has a great sense of humor. Today Scott had him zooming over the ground — horizontal in his arms — chasing the Christmas Dog. Every time they'd start towards Christmas, Andrew would look like a wrestler about to go into a match, then when he'd get close to Christmas he'd start laughing gleefully. He was having so much fun.

***

July 4, 1992

Andrew is crawling now! He's a little dynamo! He takes these short, quick, mechanical little thrusts forward with his knees. And he stood on his own today.

Everyone wants to hold him. I'm constantly being told what an adorable child he is.

The other day he played with me by sticking his pacifier in my mouth, watching me suck on it, and pulling the pacifier out again. He grinned when he did this. It was a game.

***

July 22, 1992
Andrew loves Christmas Dog! He squeals every time he sees her. He also grins when he sees me with lemonade and when I take out my guitar — two of his favorite things.

***

July 27, 1992
Drew is just a little ball of energy — rolling, crawling, standing, laughing, grinning, non-stop. He scratches surfaces to get their feel, tries to eat everything, covets whatever I'm eating and drinking, loves to bam the piano, and won't sit still long enough for me to read a story to him. Besides when he's asleep, the only time he's really quiet and still is when we're on a walk or a hike.

***

August 24, 1992
This was the last day of my time off with Andrew. My last day with Andrew all to myself. We went for walks all morning — walked up Jones Creek twice and down it thrice. Smells of an early autumn — dried leaves, blackberries. Leaves crackling against each other. It was a beautiful day! Ah! The richness and fullness of God!

The last eight and a half months since Andrew was born have just gone by in a blur — where did the time go? I try to think back on the high points of the last months: Andrew grinning love at me from a shopping cart, Andrew putting his forehead against mine, Andrew reaching out for me, Andrew coming to me when he's hurt. Andrew needing me.

I have it all — a job, a precious baby, a home, and a husband. Thank you, God, for all blessings!

***

BLESSINGS:

August 25, 1992
Andrew, our days of sleeping in are over.

ALEXANDER RAYMOND DEE TERRELL

✻✻✻

"O gentle presence, peace and joy and power;
O Life divine, that owns each waiting hour,
Thou Love that guards the nestling's faltering flight!
Keep Thou my child on upward wing tonight."
From the *Christian Science Hymnal*, words by Mary Baker Eddy

✻✻✻

I'd hoped that with the birth of my second child I would have a full night's sleep before going into labor (having experienced a sleepless night in the birth of my first son) and that, unlike my first birthing experience, this time the process would be quick and easy. Having taken no pain medication in the birth of my first son, I'd also decided that I would ask for an epidural with this one, reasoning that even Christian Scientists usually get Novocain before letting dentists drill their teeth.

It all began as I'd hoped it would. I got my full night's sleep, started feeling labor pains at nine in the morning, and, according to the midwife who met my husband and I at the hospital, was proceeding very smoothly and quickly through the birth. I asked for the epidural and was given one. Life was looking pretty good. Even the nurse attending me commented on how great it was to have a nice, normal couple to work with and to have a nice, normal birth to witness.

But not long after I was given the epidural, something started to go wrong. Apparently the baby's cord was wrapped around his neck and he was in distress. It was decided to give me a caesarean section to get the baby out quickly.

As they wheeled me down to the operating room (my rear sticking up in the air in a very undignified position), I called back to my mom, who was following behind the gurney, to phone the Christian

Science practitioner at the Christian Science Reading Room and ask her to pray for us.

Once they got me down to the O.R. I was attached to machines to monitor the baby's heart rate and blood pressure, the staff took Scott away to don him in surgical garb, and the surgical team prepared to slice me open. Everything was happening very quickly, and there was a lot of bustling activity surrounding me, but, strangely, I felt very calm. I knew that no matter what happened, God was in control and the baby was moving at His direction and guidance.

Now I was surrounded by a team of medical staffers whom, aside from my midwife, I'd never before met. Their eyes flicked from the monitor to my belly and back to the monitor again. I saw they were all puzzled by something. There was a moment of quiet. Then suddenly they all began yelling, "Push! Push!" – like they were spectators at a sporting event. I felt surrounded in Love – love from the medical staff who only wanted the best for my baby, love from my husband, and love from God. In a matter of moments our son entered the world in the old-fashioned way and the medical staff whooped like their favorite team had just won the championship. One of the nurses was crying. When I asked her why, she said that as an operating room nurse she'd never before been able to witness a baby being born naturally, and she felt she'd just witnessed a rare and special thing.

When I asked my midwife what had happened that had enabled my son to be born without a caesarean section, she said, "We don't know."

Later my mom shared what the Christian Science practitioner had told her when she reached her on the phone: "Life loves that baby!"

***

For a few hours we called our son Pieter Dee. Then we tried out the name Nicholas Piet. Finally, after a day in his company, we realized that this baby had big presence – his body was small, but something of his irrepressible identity was communicating itself to us—and we knew he needed a big name to match that identity. So we named him Alexander Raymond Dee Terrell. His name had more syllables than he had poundage, but it fit him just right all the same.

LOST AND FOUND

"For there is nothing covered, that shall not be revealed;
neither hid, that shall not be known."
Luke 12: 2

✳✳✳

I was visiting a friend of mine from college and we decided to go for a walk on a dirt road near her house. It was a gusty day, the wind whipping against us as we forged down the road. A speck of dust blew into my eye and settled on my contact lens. Ordinarily, on a windy day like this, I would have just endured the discomfort. But that speck of dust was driving me nuts. I pulled the corner of my eyelid and popped the contact into my hand at the exact moment that a particularly strong gust of wind hit me. The wind picked the contact lens off my palm and carried it away.

I looked down the road, which stretched for miles, and turned to my friend. "Kathy," I said, not sure whether to laugh or cry, "My contact lens just blew away."

She turned and looked at me, her eyebrows raised. There was a moment's pause as she processed this news. "Okay," she said, "Let's find it."

The outcome looked bleak. The contact lens could be anywhere in a five mile radius. But we decided to give it the old college try. At first our search was haphazard. Then Kathy said, "There's got to be a scientific way of doing this."

Scientific. Christianly Scientific. I began to pray.

I knew that nothing could be lost to God, nothing could be outside His consciousness. He knew where everything was and I just needed to listen to Him.

I looked down on the ground in front of my feet and my contact lens winked up at me! I can't describe the joy of finding that little piece of glass. Finding my contact lens was, I had no doubt, another amazing proof of God's care for me.

***

Several years later I had another incredible experience with a lost contact lens.

I'd somehow managed to lose a contact in the living room this time. My little boy wanted to help me find it and asked me what it looked like. I told him it was a tiny little piece of plastic. He lifted up the cushions of the sofa, took a peek, and said, "Like this?" He'd found the contact lens that he'd accidentally knocked out of my eye the year before! Like the one I had just lost, this contact was for my left eye. I never found the other one, but I stuck the one Andrew found in my eye, and I was good to go!

***

On one of our trips back east I'd insisted that Scott and I make a pilgrimage to Ben and Jerry's ice cream factory in Vermont. Scott didn't want to spend a lot of time there — we had places to go and people to see and were on a tight schedule — but we zipped in long enough to buy some New York Super Fudge Chunk and snap some pictures.

A couple of hours and about a hundred miles later we were unpacking the car to carry our things into the New Hampshire motel where we were going to spend the night, when Scott noticed his camera bag was missing. All in a flash it came to him where he had left the bag: In the restroom at Ben and Jerry's!

Losing a camera is a big deal. Losing a camera when your livelihood depends upon it is beyond big. Scott made his living as a newspaper photographer and he needed that camera bag to continue to do his job.

I called a Christian Science friend to help support us in prayer. Scott and I went to bed, but by 5:30 we were up — neither one of us able to sleep. We decided to drive back to Ben and Jerry's right then.

It was an other-worldly journey. (I'm not going to use the word "mystical" here — because that implies there were secrets and unknowns and mysteries. Nor will I use the word "magical" — as that implies something supernatural at work. In Christian Science I've come to believe that the realm and power of Spirit is neither mysterious nor supernatural, but the only reality, and completely natural.)

We hit the road before the sun rose, in that pre-dawn time of the day when all the colors are muted to pink and gray and there is incredible peace and beauty. I remember feeling an absolute certainty that Life is wholly good and that everything is as it should be, and all of God's children moving in harmony with one another. I had no doubt that we would find Scott's cameras.

Scott was concerned that somebody might have found his camera bag and kept it. But I had a clear sense of the honesty of all of God's children. I sang softly to myself these words from a song in the *Christian Science Hymnal* (words by Emily F. Seal), "Thou art Truth's honest child, of pure and sinless heart. Thou treadest undefiled in Christly paths apart. Vain dreams shall disappear as Truth dawns on the sight; The phantoms of thy fear shall flee before the light."

We arrived at Ben and Jerry's about 7:30. It wasn't yet open for the tourists, but a few of the workers were arriving and heading into the ice cream factory. One of these workers was getting out of his car as we pulled in next to him. While Scott stayed in the car — too traumatized by the loss of his cameras to move—I walked up to the worker, introduced myself, and explained our situation.

The man was very kind and volunteered to let me into the factory to see if I could find the camera bag. As we walked down the road to Ben and Jerry's he asked me if I'd been able to get a tour of the factory the day before and I told him no, we'd been in too much of a rush. So after he let me into the factory, he quickly gave me my own private tour. I was in Karen-heaven.

At the end of my tour he walked up to the information counter, knelt down behind it, and cheerfully plucked out Scott's camera bag from the lost and found. There was a card from a seafood restaurant in Boston attached to the camera bag, and the name of the man who had found the bag and brought it to the lost and found. It was an Italian name, I remember, and I vowed to write a thank you note to that wonderful finder of lost camera bags, but I lost the card before I could write the note — so if you're reading this and you're the one who found my husband's cameras back in the summer of 1993 — I thank you!

I told my tour guide that he was truly an angel and thanked him profusely.

As I neared our car Scott looked up. He saw the camera bag and began crying.

For me, this experience was another proof of the power of God, Good, in our lives.

CAR STORIES

✵✵✵

"Accidents are unknown to God, or immortal Mind, and we must
leave the mortal basis of belief and unite with the one Mind, in
order to change the notion of chance to the proper sense of God's
unerring direction and thus bring out harmony."
From *Science and Health with Key to the Scriptures*
by Mary Baker Eddy

✵✵✵

I am not a car person. Unlike my sons and husband, I have no
sense of car styles or makes and, until a year ago, had never owned a
new car in my life.

A year ago I was driving home from my Wednesday church tes-
timony meeting where I'd conducted the church service as First Reader. I always feel safe when I'm coming home from church – protected
because I've been about doing "God's business." So when the voice in
my head said, "You need to get off the exit here. Your car is going to
break down," I argued with it.

"That's nonsense!" I asserted. "I'm not going to accept that!"
and kept driving.

When I approached the next exit, the voice again directed me to
exit. I, again, argued with it.

Right after passing that exit my car began to rattle and shake.

"Crap!"

I was wearing a dress and church shoes. I had no cell phone. It
was getting dark outside. It did not seem to me a good time to pull
over to the shoulder of the freeway and begin to walk. So I kept driving. The rattling grew more alarming. My car began to reduce speed
– from 70 mph to 50 to 40. Humbled, I prayed. "God, I know I
should have listened to your voice! Please just get me to the next exit
and let me get to a phone!"

By the time my car reached the exit it was going 35 mph. When the car reached the top of the exit, the engine light went on and the car died. But I had just enough speed to turn right and coast down to the gas station to use the phone there.

***

The mechanic told my husband and me that the timing belt on the car had come loose and whipped around inside the engine, destroying it (the irony here is that Scott and I had made an appointment to have the timing belt replaced in a few days' time). It would cost $2000 to replace the engine.

Traumatized by my adventure on the freeway, my reaction to this news was to just want to get rid of the car. Scott said, "That car gave its life for you," and tried to convince me to replace the engine, but I would have none of it.

The next day we began our search for a new used car. Not being by nature a car person, I had but four requirements for a new car: It had to have a stickshift (from much previous experience with older cars I'd learned how to start a car with standard transmission if the battery is dead or the starter won't work, and thought this a rather handy thing to be able to do); it had to get good gas mileage; it had to be able to get us into the mountains; and it had to be able to haul around a family of four, a family pet or two, and enough lumber to fence in a small garden. None of the used cars we looked at fit the bill. So finally my husband and I took the plunge and began looking at new cars. We were able to get a good deal on a new station wagon. And so, at the age of 47, for the first time in my life I became the proud owner of a spanking new automobile!

I give thanks to God for getting me safely to a phone that night when my car broke down. And, even though I didn't listen to Him, I thank Him, too, for trying to direct me to get off the freeway. The lesson here is that God is always guiding us, and it behooves us to listen.

***

BLESSINGS:

There was another time when I heard God's voice in my car and *did* listen. I was driving along a busy road in a local city and pulled into the turn lane to turn left onto another busy road. The light was red for me, so I stopped, and other cars pulled into the lane behind me to turn left, also. When the left turn light turned green I took my foot off the brake and began to pull forward. At that moment a voice said very clearly, "Stop! Look!" I immediately stopped and looked to the left. I saw a car come speeding down the hill towards the intersection. The driver zipped through the red light, looked at me, realized what she had done, opened her mouth into a perfect "O," and kept going. I realized in that moment that if I hadn't stopped she would have broad-sided my car. It was a blessing that I hadn't pulled into the intersection. It was a blessing, too, that the drivers in the cars behind me were alert and stopped when I stopped. No one was rear-ended.

✳✳✳

Have you ever seen a car dance? It's an amazing thing to witness, let me tell you.

My opportunity to witness a car dance came as I was crossing over the Tacoma Narrows Bridge one day. The Narrows Bridge is a long bridge that stretches across a part of the Puget Sound, far below. People tend to be a little wary when crossing this bridge because the lanes are narrow, there's no shoulder to pull onto, and a plunge off the bridge wouldn't be a good thing.

As I was about to leave the bridge on that particular day, I saw a VW bug approaching from the opposite direction suddenly swerve into my lane. "Accidents are unknown to God!" I affirmed loudly to myself. A moment before the bug moved into my lane the highway crossing the bridge had been busy and full of traffic, but it seemed to me the moment the driver of the VW began to lose control, all the traffic just disappeared. In retrospect, I'm guessing that all the drivers in the other cars must have calmly done what I did—I slowed and moved as far right as I could, and watched the VW fishtail a dance back and forth across three lanes. It was a rather graceful dance, really, and when he was done the driver straightened the car out and, as if nothing had happened, went on his way.

What a blessing to see such sublime evidence of God's control over Her creation — to know that all of God's children were being guided by God to move in harmony with each other — to realize that all of Her children are alert, intelligent, calm, competent.

***

One day last summer, as I was driving with my sons to visit my aunts who live 200 miles to the south of us, I was given the opportunity to witness another of God's blessings. We'd made it about two thirds of the way there, when I looked up and saw a red SUV in the opposite lanes suddenly smash into the freeway divider and begin to climb over it into my lane. I slowed down, but couldn't move away from the SUV into the right lane because there were other cars around me. The highway divider kept the other vehicle from entering my lane, but as I went past I heard a horrible grinding sound. I pulled over and ran back to see if I could help, declaring all the way, "God is your life! God is Love!"

***

As I approached the overturned SUV, I could see a hand sticking out of the car. I had a moment of fright because the hand seemed so still. But by the time I reached the vehicle other people were surrounding the driver and I saw that she was alive and appeared to be uninjured. The driver was a teenage girl and she was alone, except for a puppy.

Two or three men wrapped her in a blanket and carried her away from the crash, and a handful of us squatted down next to her. She seemed to be in shock. She was concerned about her puppy, and we all reassured her that the puppy was fine. I put my hand on her shoulder and talked to her in my chatty teacher voice — the same voice I would use to talk to my middle school students about the school dance or the weather outside. My instincts told me that the girl needed to hear a calm voice. At one point she said, "My parents are going to kill me!" and I laughed and told her that her parents were just going to be happy that she was alright.

The woman next to me seemed very efficient—she'd placed herself behind the girl and was supporting her shoulders, checking her pulse. I turned to her. "Are you a nurse?" I asked.

She smiled and said, "I graduated from nursing school just yesterday."

Wasn't that wonderful? This girl couldn't be in better human hands! And I knew that she'd never been separated from the loving arms of God.

As the ambulance pulled up, I leaned over to the girl until her eyes looked directly at me. "God bless you," I said.

Her eyes, which had seemed a little unfocused until then, suddenly focused on me. She smiled. "Thank you," she said.

I knew that was all I needed to do there, and left her in the care of the newly-graduated nurse and the paramedics.

God provides us with whatever human help we need whenever we need it, and He provides us with continual opportunity to express His love to our fellow man. For this, I am grateful.

FURTHER PROOFS

✳✳✳

"Every day makes its demands upon us for higher proofs rather than professions of Christian power. These proofs consist solely in the destruction of sin, sickness, and death by the power of Spirit, as Jesus destroyed them. This is an element of progress, and progress is the law of God, whose law demands of us only what we can certainly fulfil."
From *Science and Health with Key to the Scriptures* by Mary Baker Eddy

✳✳✳

Just before the Christmas Dog entered our lives I got myself really sick. I was working three jobs — I was on call as a substitute teacher, serving as the local high school's Saturday School teacher, and tutoring high schoolers in the evenings through an alternative high school program. I felt myself growing more and more tired as the school year progressed and by December I was exhausted and coughing a deep raspy cough almost non-stop. I never visited a doctor about this, but several people suggested to me that it sounded like I had a bad case of bronchitis.

I finally had to quit the tutoring gig and began to spend that "extra time" in the evenings praying about my situation. At first my prayers involved an intellectual study of the *Scriptures* and the Christian Science textbook. But I didn't seem to be making any progress with this illness. I don't mean to sound melodramatic here, but the thought did occur to me that I might die from this thing.

One evening I was freezing cold so I put on my down climbing parka and a wool hat, and Scott got the woodstove going full blast for me before going outside to chop more wood. I sat in my rocking chair, going back and forth, back and forth, and lamenting my woeful situation to myself in between coughs.

Suddenly I stopped rocking. I got a vision of how I must look — down parka, wool hat, rocking back and forth, coughing, and muttering to myself — and I burst out laughing. "This is absolutely ridiculous!" I shouted. "I'm done with this!" And I stood up, took off the parka and hat, and went into the kitchen to make dinner. I was healed.

***

When Alexander was a couple of months old he came down with an ear infection. As per Scott's wishes, I took him to a doctor who gave me a prescription for an antibiotic. I faithfully administered that antibiotic to my baby for the required ten days and witnessed no improvement in his condition. I admit to feeling relieved when we finally ran out of the medicine.

Now it was my turn to use the method of healing I'd always relied on.

I called a Christian Science practitioner for prayerful support and carried Xander out to the back steps to sit in the sun with him. I sang hymns from the *Christian Science Hymnal* and, looking at his precious little face, knew him as God's perfect reflection of good. He fell asleep in my arms and the ear infection disappeared.

***

When Andrew was twelve he hurt his knee high-jumping. I took him to the doctor who told us that Andrew had "Jumper's Knee" and should curtail his activities for a couple of months. Andrew snorted and I knew he was thinking, "Yeah, right, like that's going to happen!" I brought him home. There was no curtailing of activities. In a matter of days his knee was fine. When I asked him how his knee had healed so fast, he looked at me with his eyebrows raised and said, "Well, duh, Mom. Christian Science!"

***

I have this incredible dynamo of a friend named Teresa. Teresa and I were teaching partners for five years — she taught Science and

Math to our group of eighth graders, and I taught Language Arts and Social Studies. We were a good team, I think, and found we had a lot in common—among other things we both were born in September; both of us were the oldest of three children, with two younger brothers; both of us owned old VW beetles as our first cars; we both graduated from Washington State University; I conceived my eldest son the day hers was born; and we both came to work at Allen School the same year.

Teresa is a wonder. She's fast-talking, witty, intense, passionate about what's important to her, and spiritually focused on her Christian faith. When she learned I was a Christian Scientist, she was intrigued by the notion that I depend on God for healing, and asked a lot of questions. In recent years she's sometimes called me and asked me to help her pray about something.

During one of these calls she explained that there was a man who taught with her at the high school who was told he probably had cancer, but was going in for a final definitive exam. Would I join her in prayer for her friend? She said this man didn't really believe in God, but she had told him she was going to pray for him anyway and he'd laughed and agreed that, in the unlikely event his tests for cancer came back negative, he'd give more consideration to the notion of God.

I happily agreed to join in her prayers and conscientiously sat down with "my books" to heal the belief of cancer. Mary Baker Eddy writes in the Christian Science textbook, "'Agree to disagree' with approaching symptoms of chronic or acute disease, whether it is cancer, consumption, or smallpox. Meet the incipient stages of disease with as powerful mental opposition as a legislator would employ to defeat the passage of an inhuman law. Rise in the conscious strength of the spirit of Truth to overthrow the plea of mortal mind, alias matter, arrayed against the supremacy of Spirit." In the next paragraph Mrs. Eddy writes, "Instead of blind and calm submission to the incipient or advanced stages of disease, rise in rebellion against them." What power lies in those words! I knew, without doubt, that Teresa's friend was whole and healthy.

When Teresa called back in a few days she told me that the man was found to be cancer-free! Isn't God wonderful?!

THE BIG APPLE

***

"And they shall build the old wastes,
They shall raise up the former desolations,
And they shall repair the waste cities...
For thus saith the Lord,
Behold, I will extend peace to her like a river...
As one whom his mother comforteth,
So will I comfort you..."
Isaiah 61: 4; 66:13

***

On the morning of August 2, 2001, the Terrell Family descended en masse onto the streets of New York City. It had taken a plane, a car, and a train to get us here from Bow, Washington. We hit the streets running, not wanting to waste a single moment of our one day in the Big Apple.

As you already know, Scott had been raised on the east coast, and so he'd visited New York now and then as a youth, and I had been to the city once years before. But our teen-age niece, Katie, and our sons, Andrew and Alexander, had never been witness to this amazing city, and I was determined that they have the full New York experience.

We'd hoped to catch a Broadway matinee, but matinees don't happen in New York on Thursdays. So we decided to spend our day visiting the typical tourist spots: the Statue of Liberty, Empire State Building, Times Square, and Godiva's Chocolates.

From the moment nine year-old Andrew hit the streets of New York he was grinning. He loved the energy, the pace, and the crazy antics of the city's residents. He held the hand of the beautiful Blue Lady — a living statue in Battery Park, reverently dropped coins into the case of a gifted saxophonist jamming on a street corner, and watched in happy fascination a contortionist who was performing for the line of people waiting to get on the ferry to Liberty Island.

"You're in the city that has the best of the best," I told him. "The best musicians, the best actors, the best businessmen and writers — you'll find them here — they're walking the same streets we're walking right now." And Andrew nodded his head in excitement, that grin on his face.

Seven year-old Alexander was more reticent. He walked the streets saucer-eyed as he tried to process his New York experience. At the top of the Empire State Building he peered down onto the streets below, his eyes riveted on those bright yellow taxis — the honking from them carrying all the way up to where we perched eighty floors above. When we passed through the souvenir shop Alexander chose a model of a yellow taxi as his official souvenir, rather than his usual stuffed animal. Andrew was the one who left the gift shop with the stuffed animal. Scott and I each bought mugs with the New York skyline emblazoned on them. I think Katie bought a sweatshirt.

Pretty Katie, oblivious to her prettiness and the looks of her male peers, marched down New York's streets with an unself-conscious curiosity. Like Andrew, she, too, carried a perpetual grin on her face. Her one hope was that before the day was done we'd be able to visit Times Square.

By the time we finally made it to Times Square it was past dinnertime and we were famished. A young man magically appeared with a coupon for Planet Hollywood, a restaurant just down the street.

And this is when Alexander came to life. In the foyer of Planet Hollywood there was a mannequin garbed in a Darth Vader costume from the "Star Wars" movies. Now here was something Alexander could relate to! Here was something familiar to his world and — I know this sounds weird — homey. Suddenly he was the one with the grin on his face. "You mean this is the real costume, Mom?!" he asked, all excited. In an instant he became Luke Skywalker, in saberplay with the forces of darkness, and all was right with his world.

***

BLESSINGS:

Oh, the lovely people we met that day! There were the young women from the Bronx who sat across from us on the subway, proudly telling us about the city they'd lived in all their lives and suggesting places we should visit; the kindly chap who helped us to determine which subways we needed to ride; That wonderfully wacky family of fellow tourists we met on Liberty Island who, upon being caught hamming it up for each other, graciously agreed to continue posing as Statues of Liberty so I could snap their photo.

At the end of the day, happily tired and satiated, shopping bags full of souvenirs and stomachs full of Planet Hollywood burgers and Godiva's chocolates, we boarded the subway that would take us out of New York. As we sorted ourselves into seats, a businessman kindly offered to trade seats with me so I could sit next to Alexander. The man and I struck up conversation. I can't remember now where he worked exactly — Wall Street? The World Trade Center? But I remember I enjoyed talking with him and thought, once again, how fine are the people of New York City. Before I got off the subway I gave him my subway card, which still had about $10 worth of subway rides on it. I told him I was leaving to go back to Seattle in a couple of days and wouldn't have any use for it. He smiled and thanked me. We shook hands good-bye.

On September 11th my thoughts turned, again, to that man on the subway, and all those people I'd met in New York five weeks earlier. I found myself looking at the skyline depicted on my souvenir mug and realizing, in shock, that skyline no longer existed. And, like others, I prayed.

As I prayed it became clear to me that nothing could destroy what is good about New York — the vitality and spirit and life that was expressed in The Big Apple couldn't be lost.

***

Two years later Scott and I again took our sons to New York City. This time we planned it so that we'd be there on a Wednesday to see the Broadway matinee show of "Thoroughly Modern Milly."

On the train ride out we talked to a woman who had lost friends on 9-11. What struck me about this woman was her attitude of solemn purpose. We were to witness this attitude a lot throughout our day in New York City.

When we got off our train at Grand Central Station we saw that National Guards troops had been added to the station since the last time we were there. It was rather strange to eat at a lunch counter in the Station while uniformed men with rifles stood on guard behind us. I'll confess that at first it freaked me out a little bit. But as soon as I said "Hi" to a guardsman and got a smile and a "Good morning!" in return, I felt better.

New York had changed in many ways since we'd last been there and not all of the changes were necessarily bad ones. One of the things I'd enjoyed about the city before was the edge it had to it – I'd always sort of gotten a kick out of that aggressive, rude quality that I'd seen in the street vendors the two previous times I'd been to the Big Apple. To me, that was a part of New York and I couldn't imagine it would be as fun without it. But it seemed to me that edginess was gone now. Even the street vendors were patient and courteous. And I found I actually kind of liked it.

People still moved at a fast pace, but the aggressiveness was gone. Maybe 9-11 had given the people of New York a different set of priorities. I don't know. It's possible my perception of post-9-11 New York is totally bogus. But it seemed to me that if 9-11 had tested the resolve and courage of New York's inhabitants, they'd passed the test, and had come out of it wiser and kinder and better. Generalizations, of course. But that's my perception.

***

"Thoroughly Modern Milly" was great fun! Even Andrew and Alexander got caught up in the music and plot.

At the intermission Alexander and I went down to look in the orchestra pit. It wasn't what I'd expected. I'd thought I would see a semi-circle of professional musicians in tuxedoes all facing a director and looking, well, very professional. But what I saw was a group of separate cubicles with TV monitors to allow the musicians to watch the stage and an assortment of mostly abandoned instruments. It was all very casual. I think I remember seeing pop cans and snacks in the cubicles, like you would find in most any office.

There were still a few musicians in the orchestra pit and Alexander and I chatted with them a bit about what it was like to be a Broadway musician. Just as we were about to go back to our seats one of the musicians said, "Wait a minute!" and reached down to pull up some slips of paper from the pit floor. "These are the return tickets that Milly tears up and throws away at the beginning of the show," he explained, and handed them to us as souvenirs.

"Wow! Thank you!" I said, awe-struck. I was actually holding a prop that a Broadway actress and a Broadway musician had touched before me! Life doesn't get much better than that. Those slips of paper were, for me, a blessing.

***

After the show I somehow managed to persuade my men-folk to escort me to Tiffany's. I didn't have a lot of time to waste there, so I asked one of the Tiffany's employees to direct me to the counter appropriate for my financial situation (the cheap counter). The gentleman who served me was a hoot! I didn't feel the need to try to pretend to be something I'm not. (I mean really, who am I going to fool anyway?) I confirmed for him what I'm sure he already knew — I was a tourist looking for something inexpensive to bring home as a souvenir from Tiffany's. The counter was lined with patrons wanting help, all probably willing to buy something bigger and pricier than me, but the gentleman behind the counter smiled a genuinely warm smile at me and took his time helping me — just as if I was one of those wealthy customers that steps into Tiffany's on a regular basis. In the end I picked an Italian necklace with a silver teardrop hanging from it. As my "consultant" carefully placed it in its own turquoise-colored leather pouch, in its own turquoise-colored shiny bag, he told me that the designer had said whoever wore this necklace would never cry.

"Except for joy, right?" I asked.

He grinned, "That goes without saying."

The necklace was beautiful, but the best thing about walking into Tiffany's was meeting the nice people who worked there.

***

New York City is still home to the "best of the best" — the best musicians, actors, writers, businessmen, and jewelers, too.

GARDEN BLESSINGS

***

"And the Lord shall guide thee continually, and satisfy they soul in
drought,
and make fat thy bones: and thou shalt be like a watered garden,
and like a spring of water, whose waters fail not."
Isaiah 58: 11

***

There are lessons to be learned in gardening. And lessons are
blessings.

I get great joy from imagining my gardens before I've actually
begun planting them. I am currently (and maybe forever?) at work
creating my "Secret Garden," which lies about fifty paces behind our
home. A plant has to be more than pretty to make it into the Secret
Garden. It has to have something else going for it: Maybe it has a
lovely fragrance (I'm big into smells), or it attracts butterflies or hum-
mingbirds, or it was given me by a special friend.

I started my Secret Garden three years ago with a mock orange tree, a rosa rugosa, and a couple of tulip bulbs. It's now surrounded on three sides by a split rail cedar fence (which I put in myself), and on the fourth side by a wild hedge planted for the purpose
of enticing the birds. The hedge contains wild rose, "twin flowers,"
and snowberry bushes, as well as other natural flora that I've dug up
from along roadsides in the last three years. Joining my tulips, mock
orange, and rosa rugosa, my garden now includes lilacs, an old-fashioned "Cecil Bruner" climbing rose (which I dug up from my mom's
garden, and has been in the family for at least 40 years), a couple of
butterfly bushes, a baby wisteria, some forsythia, phlox, a honeysuckle
azalea (glorious smell!) and two other azaleas given me by friends,
laurel, honeysuckle climbing a trellis, purple scabiosa (it attracts but-

terflies), a flowering quince, foxglove, a sweet-smelling daphne, some lupine and delphinium, hollyhocks and crocosmia. I've gotten a little carried away.

The imagining, choosing, and planting of the plants is great fun. It's the nurturing of the plants and the weeding around them once they're planted that tests my dedication.

On page 343 of Mary Baker Eddy's *Miscellaneous Writings*, she writes, "Warmed by the sunshine of Truth, watered by the heavenly dews of Love, the fruits of Christian Science spring upward, and away from the sordid soil of self and matter. Are we clearing the gardens of thought by uprooting the noxious weeds of passion, malice, envy, and strife?" She goes on to write, "The weeds of mortal mind are not always destroyed by the first uprooting; they reappear, like devastating witch-grass, to choke the coming clover. O stupid gardener! Watch their reappearing, and tear them away from their native soil, until no seedling be left to propagate – and rot."

I can't tell you the number of times I have muttered to myself under my breath, "O stupid gardener!" as I've impatiently tugged on a weed and felt its root snap in the ground. If a gardener doesn't dig up the whole root the blasted weed will come back. So there is great satisfaction for me in digging deeper and deeper until I yank up a root a foot long. Some ruthless hunter-instinct comes out in me as my hands relentlessly go for that tap root. One time I pulled out a dandelion root that was three feet long! – I wanted to mount it on my wall in the same way a fisherman mounts his swordfish or a hunter mounts his moose head. But I figured a mounted root on my wall wouldn't have the same effect as a stuffed swordfish (although, to be honest, a mounted root actually makes more sense to me than a mounted moose head) and it may establish me for sure as the neighborhood eccentric.

I like the analogy Mary Baker Eddy makes between gardening and cleaning the "noxious weeds" out of one's thought. Keeping my thoughts properly nurtured and tended is as much a workout as tending my Secret Garden, and absolutely more important.

***

BLESSINGS:

On my daily walks of five years ago I use to pass this beautiful yard that looked like a park. There were islands of flowers everywhere, all aesthetically placed and pleasing to the eye. It was obvious that the hand of a professional was at work there. But for months I never saw anyone actually working in the garden. I was intrigued.

The flowers that most caught my eye in this garden were the long sprays of flame-orange crocosmia that shot out of the islands. I'd never seen this type of plant before – or if I had, I'd never noticed it – but they were hard to miss in this garden. I found myself lusting after them.

Weeks went by and the crocosmia were on their last legs when I finally met the owner of the garden. She was directing a handful of children in the weeding of her garden when I first saw her. She was pretty, lively, and had an aura of positive energy about her, and she was directing her child-helpers from a wheelchair. I walked up to her, shook her hand, introduced myself, and told her I'd been admiring her bright orange flowers for weeks. Laughing, she agreed that they were, indeed, beautiful. She told me they were called "crocosmia" and generously offered to give me some bulbs in the autumn. She didn't have to offer twice. She gave me her card – I learned she worked at the University of Washington – and told me to call her in October and she'd dig some bulbs up for me.

When October came I was too shy to call. So I just kept walking by her house, hoping she would see me and recognize me. This was a long shot, I knew. This woman was a busy lady and probably met a lot of people on a daily basis – if she even remembered who I was it would be a miracle.

But, as we learn in Christian Science, miracles (or rather natural goodnesses) do happen! There came a day when the garden lady was out in her yard as I walked by. She looked up, immediately recognized me, and told me that now was the perfect time to dig up some crocosmia bulbs. I came home from that walk with a plastic bag brimming with bulbs, feeling like I'd just robbed a candy store.

When we moved to Bow several years later and built our new house, I planted those bulbs in my Secret Garden. Every time they bloom I think of that pretty lady with the lively spirit, and her generosity to me.

***

When my boys were about two and four we'd sometimes take a one-mile jaunt around the block to get acquainted with our neighborhood. We got to know some wonderful people on these walks—the "Sports Family," which included boys my own sons' ages, the "lock and key man," the high school teacher, the man who ran the local auto repair shop, and one of our favorite people—"The Flower Man."

The Flower Man lived in a teensy little cottage on a teensy little lot, but his property was amazing for the beauteous flowers sprouting out of every square inch of dirt. He had pansies, larkspur, marigolds, delphiniums, begonias, clematis, primroses, petunias, lupines – pretty much every type of plant known to man.

As with the "Crocosmia Lady," we became acquainted with the man's garden before we became acquainted with the man himself. But there came a day when we saw the man unloading yet more flowers from the back of his truck, and we waved to him and told him how much we enjoyed his garden. He came up to talk to us then. He was a bearded man about forty, with a friendly smile and a twinkle in his eyes, and he chatted with the boys for awhile about flowers. It turns out he worked for a nursery and was often given surplus plants, which explained the profusion of flowers at his domicile. Before we continued on our walk, he gave each of the boys a pansy plant of their own to plant in our backyard.

After that, whenever we saw him in his yard on our walks, the boys would wave and yell, "Hi Mr. Flower Man!" and he would wave back with a smile on his face.

I don't know if we ever actually learned his name, but I remember feeling like a good friend had gone when he moved from the neighborhood a year or two later.

***

When we sold the house next door to our new home, we sold it to Garden People, thus ensuring that we would have Garden People for neighbors. Diana is an amazing artist with plants, and like "The Flower Man" and the "Crocosmia Lady," she is very generous. In fact, just last week I received a giant clump of tangerine-colored lilies from her.

***

My Secret Garden is full of memories and love. Everywhere I look I see my friends. At the entrance to my garden is the "Mom's Garden" plaque given me by my friend, Maria Rafaelita Christina Valdez, and a little further into the garden is the hand-made arbor she gave me. Climbing the arbor is the Cecil Bruner rose I dug up from Mom's garden, and not far away from that is the rose bush Lori (whom we're all agreed should have been born a country garden lady in Victorian England) gave me. In one corner of the garden is the lilac bush Scott gave me one Mother's Day, and in another corner is the azalea bush given me by a teacher-friend. I've planted my crocosmia from the "Crocosmia Lady" under the ash tree, and the wildflowers from the wildflower seed my mom gave me are thriving.

Such blessings!

***

Garden People are the nicest kind of people. They are nurturers, artists, lovers of God's creation. They are "the meek" from Jesus' Beatitutudes: "Blessed are the meek, for they shall inherit the earth."

***

One morning last summer, unable to sleep, I went out at four in the morning to water my Secret Garden. There were still stars in the sky when I went out. Gradually the sky began to get lighter. Birds replaced the bats. A hummingbird perched on a branch of the ash tree, watching me, as I moved the hose from plant to plant.

As I watched the last star fade in the sky, the stage began to get busy with birds swooping and chirping, and slugs hurrying home from their feast. All Creation seemed to be in anticipation mode —

waiting for the curtain to open on the new day and the Sun to enter, Stage East. It was magical to witness. A gift. I could almost hear the Creator's actors calling to one another in excitement, "Hurry! The new day's almost started!" It seemed as if all of God's creation was waiting for the play to begin — all the backstage crew rushing around to make sure the props were in place, all the actors rushing to their spots, waiting for their cues.

***

"This is the day the Lord hath made;
Be glad, give thanks, rejoice;
Stand in His presence unafraid, In praise lift up your voice.
All perfect gifts are from above, And all our blessings show
The amplitude of God's dear love,
Which every heart may know."
Christian Science Hymnal, words by L.L.R.

FEARGNORANCE

***

"There is no fear in love;
but perfect love casteth out fear..."
I John 4: 18

***

"The weapons of bigotry, ignorance, envy,
fall before an honest heart".
From *Science and Health with Key to the Scriptures*
by Mary Baker Eddy

***

Fear and ignorance always seem to go together, don't they? It's my belief that when you come to understand other people's religions, you're less likely to fear the people or the religion. I'm a great believer in the importance of trying to understand how other people think and feel and perceive the world.

One time I asked my eighth grade Social Studies students to help me list all the people who have ever had prejudice shown against them. We came up with a staggering list: People of Asian descent; People of African descent; People of Jewish descent; People of Irish descent; People of Italian descent; Hispanic people; Catholics; Protestants; Mormons; Jehovah's Witnesses; Puritans; Quakers; women; white men; gays; Native Americans; the elderly; people with weight problems; teenagers; homeless people – the list went on and on.

Then one of my students raised her hand and said, "How about Christian Scientists?"

"Yes," I said, trying not to show my surprise that this child had even heard of Christian Science, let alone might be savvy to the fact that Christian Scientists have had prejudice shown against them. "I once heard someone on a talk show say that all the Christian Scientists should be lined up and shot." My student nodded her head, like she wasn't surprised by this, and my class continued its discussion about prejudice.

After the other students had left the class I asked my student how she'd heard about Christian Science and she told me her grandmother, whom she was very close to, was a Christian Scientist. I then shared with my student that I, too, was a Christian Scientist, and she seemed pleased to hear this.

The truth is that I did once hear someone say on a local talk show that all "Christian Scientists should be lined up and shot." I'll be honest here; it was chilling to hear someone I'd never met wish me dead.

***

Many years ago I had a job working for a small business as a dispatcher/reservation clerk/payroll/accounts payable/accounts receivable person. The woman who owned the business with her husband was a devout Christian. For many months we exchanged ideas about the *Scriptures*, talked about the teachings of Jesus, and even prayed together when she was challenged with a health problem. I enjoyed our talks, and was impressed by the strength and sincerity of her religious convictions.

But my instincts told me that my employer was not ready to hear I was a Christian Scientist, so whenever she would ask me about my church affiliation, I would just say that I went to a small Christian church in a neighboring community.

There came a night, though, when my employer and a friend from her church and I were all working on inventory and accounts together, and my employer asked me, "So what church do you go to, Karen?" and I answered, "The Christian Science church in Mount Vernon."

Oh my goodness! The temperature in that room literally dropped 10 degrees! I had my back to my employer and when I turned around

I saw her mouth the words, "I didn't know!" to her friend. I think I knew right then that my days in her employee were numbered.

The next day when I came in to work I saw that she had *The Kingdom of the Cults* lying on her desk. This did not bode well. *The Kingdom of the Cults* is a classic piece of "Christian" literature, its purpose being to "expose" all the evil cults lurking in the shadows – Christian Science being one of the chief culprits.

I don't recall now how it got to this point, but I heard myself saying to her, "I think you think I'm going to hell."

This sort of threw her for a loop. Looking back, I can only imagine how confused the dear woman must have been! Here I was, the woman with whom for months she'd been praying and talking about Jesus—and my church was listed as a cult in the book she considered the authority on cults! She began talking about the prayerful support I'd given her while she was sick, the wonderful discussions we'd had about the *Bible*, and asking me if my God was the same God of "Abraham and Isaac" that she worshipped. I assured her that I worshipped that very same God. But I could tell she no longer trusted me.

A few weeks later she took me out to lunch and said, "I had this dream that a little fox was invading my home and God told me to throw that fox out of my home, so I took that fox by the scruff of the neck and threw him out of my home, and Karen, I'm going to have to let you go."

I'd seen this coming, of course. I had, in fact, been praying that God would lift me out of this unhappy work situation. So it was with a feeling of great relief that I said to my employer, "That's alright. I think we've both learned a lot in the last year." We shook hands and civilly parted company.

In the following week I continued to pray about this situation, though, feeling that it wasn't quite resolved yet in my own thoughts. I prayed to know my employer as God's child, His reflection of Love, no less loved than He loves me. I prayed to know myself as Love's reflection, too.

A week later I returned to bring back a shirt that belonged to the business. My employer's husband told me that he knew his wife would like to see me and told me where I could find her. When she saw me she smiled warmly and told me there was something she needed to say to me. She began by apologizing to me for letting me go and then she said that in the last week one of the representatives of her church, Jimmy Swaggert, had fallen in disgrace and she'd come to realize that she needed to "clean out" her "own house" before she tried to clean out someone else's house.

I recognized how hard it must have been for her to speak those words. I recognized, too, God's hand in this loving outreach from her, and we were able to part as friends.

As Mary Baker Eddy says in *Science and Health*, "…Love is reflected in love…"

Amen.

MENTAL MALPRACTICE

✳✳✳

"Christian Scientists, be a law to yourselves that mental malpractice
cannot harm you either when asleep or when awake."
From *Science and Health with Key to the Scriptures*
by Mary Baker Eddy

✳✳✳

There was a night some time ago when I was overcome with feelings of depression. I felt like I was in a deep, dark hole, and I couldn't see how I was going to get out of it. Anyone who's ever experienced depression doesn't need me to describe it. Let's just say I was in a "really bad place."

Without going into huge and specific detail, I think I need to share a bit about the circumstances that had brought me to this unhappy place. At the time there were two or three people in my life who seemed to be very critical of me. My motives were constantly being questioned, I seemed to always be in a position where I needed to defend myself, and I had to continually censor what I said, in fear that my words would get twisted around to better fit the perception these others had of me. I'm pretty sure some of you reading this can relate. I know I'm not the only one to ever go through this kind of experience. In any case, that day one of these people had told me that "everybody" was talking about me, and I'd come home that night feeling a real sense of self-worthlessness. I was becoming convinced that I *was* a bad person. I'd begun to believe the negative perceptions about me. If "everybody" believed these horrible things about me they must be true.

I was serving as First Reader in my church at this time, and one of my responsibilities was to put together readings from the *Bible* the Christian Science textbook for our Wednesday night meetings.

The thought came to me that I needed to put together readings on "Mental Malpractice." If you're not familiar with the term "mental malpractice," just conjure up the concept of *medical* malpractice and then imagine someone committing malpractice against another person using their thoughts rather than medicine. Mental malpractice can be committed against another person unintentionally or with deliberation.

What came to me when I was in the grip of this depression was that I was being unintentionally mentally malpracticed. But I knew, too, that Christian Science had given me the tools to protect myself from it.

I thought about Job in the *Bible*. Now there was a man who was mentally malpracticed!

Remember Job's three "friends" – Eliphaz, Bildad, and Zophar? Mental malpractioners, all of them! Eliphaz "comforts" Job in his time of affliction by telling him, "…who ever perished, being innocent? Or where were the righteous cut off? Even as I have seen, they that plow iniquity, and sow wickedness, reap the same."

Bildad says, "If thou were pure and upright; surely now he (God) would awake for thee, and make the habitation of thy righteousness prosperous."

And Zophar gives these reassuring words to Job, "But oh that God would speak, and open his lips against thee; And that he would shew thee the secrets of wisdom, that they are double to that which is! Know therefore that God exacteth of thee less than thine iniquity deserveth."

All three of these men saw Job as full of iniquity and deserving of the grief that's come upon him. All three of these men accredit God with the evil that's befallen Job. And all three of these men are having great fun picking Job apart when he's down, and setting themselves up as experts on his identity.

But I love how Job answers them, "No doubt but ye are the people, and wisdom shall die with you. But I have understanding as well as you; I am not inferior to you…Surely I would speak to the Almighty, and I desire to reason with God. But ye are forgers of lies, ye are all physicians of no value. O that ye would altogether hold your peace! and it would be your wisdom. Will ye speak wickedly for God? and talk deceitfully for him? will ye contend for God?"

And then the Lord says to Eliphaz, "My wrath is kindled against thee, and against thy two friends: for ye have not spoken of me the thing that is right, as my servant Job hath."

"And the Lord turned the captivity of Job, when he prayed for his friends: also the Lord gave Job twice as much as he had before," the story ends.

I love that Job prayed for his friends after they had spoken like that to him! I suppose his friends were under the grip of mental malpractice themselves, if they were seeing Job the way they were.

I realized, as I read about Job, that, like him, I was God's loved and loving child, and not this other identity that others were trying to attach to me. As my friend, Maria Rafaelita Christina Valdez, says, "Just because somebody calls you a chair, doesn't make you a chair." Words of wisdom!

Well, in putting together my readings I felt a real sense of peace about it all. I decided that the next day I would just "shine my light" on these people. And that's what I did.

At the end of the day somebody left me a note that told me not "everybody" was seeing me in the negative way I'd been told "everybody" was seeing me. In fact, my anonymous note-writer was very angry that she and others had been mentioned to me as my critics by a person who was basically only speaking for himself and two other persons.

That felt good.

Several days later the man who'd told me "everybody" was talking about me stopped by to see how I was doing. Now he might have done this because he knew I was "wise" to him and he was a little worried about what I was going to do about it. I prefer to think, though, that he was genuinely feeling remorse for what he'd said to me.

***

I've come to realize that there is no such thing as an "insurmountable" problem, that there is no such thing as "hopeless," and that life always, always gets better. I've found the most effective way for me to deal with a sense of depression is to think outside myself, do something good for somebody else, and love, love, love.

CONNECTIONS

***

"Beloved Christian Scientists, keep your mind so filled with Truth
and Love, that sin, disease, and death cannot enter them. It is plain
that nothing can be added to the mind already full. There is no
door through which evil can enter, and no space for evil to fill in a
mind filled with goodness. Good thoughts are an impervious armor;
clad therewith you are completely shielded from the attacks of error
of every sort. And not only yourselves are safe, but all whom your
thoughts rest upon are thereby benefited."
From *Prose Works* by Mary Baker Eddy

***

Can I just tell you about some of the faces I've passed on streets,
or people I've had brief contact with, who have stayed with me through
the years? I consider these people blessings to me, a small foretaste of
Heaven, a part of my mental community. And I am of the opinion
that some day I'll meet them all again and we'll get "caught up."

***

There were about four hundred people in my high school gradu-
ating class and some of these people I only knew by face, passing them
in the hall on the way to class. Out of these four hundred people we
had four black people (my high school was unfortunate in its lack of
diversity). One of these four shared my table in Home Ec class and
she kept me perpetually laughing with her dry sense of humor as we
went from one food disaster to the next. But I didn't share any classes
with the other students of African descent and never really had an
opportunity to get to know any of them.

I do remember the time, though, when I was rushing up the
stairs to get to my next class at the same time one of the two black

men in my class was rushing down them. We collided and I would have fallen backwards down the stairs for sure if he hadn't quickly grabbed onto my elbows to hold me in place. I don't remember if I ever thanked him for that – so I'll thank him now. He was my hero at that moment.

***

As I mentioned in a previous chapter, I use to work at Mount Rainier National Park in the summers between college, and I met the nicest people up there!

I remember a couple of men from Syria who wrote out their names in Syrian and then wrote a greeting to me in their language. I still have that note tucked away somewhere.

And I remember the two exceedingly handsome young men who entered the gift shop as I stood behind the counter with my friend and co-worker, Marilyn. Marilyn and I took one look at these men, turned to look at each other, and without saying a word quietly slid down behind the counter. "Did you see those guys?!" we both whispered simultaneously. We quickly composed ourselves and stood back up, only to find the two men standing on the other side of the counter, grinning at us.

It turns out they were from The Netherlands. I wrote my name, "Molenaar," on a piece of paper and handed it to them, telling them that was my name. You can't get much more Dutch than "Molenaar" (the Dutch version for "Miller") and the young men and I soon were engaged in a lively conversation about the home of my ancestors. (After they left, Marilyn turned to me and said, "Why can't I have the Dutch name?" Ah! What a blessing to be Dutch!)

***

Heathrow Airport in London is an amazing place to meet people! I remember sitting in an area within the airport, waiting for the next flight to Amsterdam, and feeling incredibly thirsty. A Britisher sat across from me with a big cup full of some cool orange drink. "Where'd you get that?" I asked, lusting after it.

"The Crush?" he asked, pointing to his drink, "It's easy to get dehydrated when you're traveling, isn't it?" He asked in his wonderful British accent, and then pointed me in the direction of "The Crush." When I came back we talked a bit as travelers do. Soon a Japanese man settled into our little nest of chairs and joined in the conversation. By this time I happened to be leafing through a London newspaper and came upon a picture of an American dignitary and a Japanese dignitary shaking hands and making amends over Pearl Harbor and Hiroshima. I pointed this out to the Japanese man and he smiled and nodded and said something like, "Good, good." It came to me then that the Britisher, the Japanese man, and myself were all holding our own peace summit right there in Heathrow Airport. (I like the idea of that — people without title or official position by-passing the politicians and meeting at Heathrow to solve the world's problems.)

Traveling through London, I had the blessing of riding on the top of a double-decker bus with a pair of dear motherly British ladies who cautioned me to be careful of strange men on my journey, and gave me tips on how to stay safe in Europe. It was like talking to two Miss Marples.

After I arrived in The Netherlands I remember the tall middle-aged Dutch businessman with glasses who kept me from getting on the wrong train (I think it was bound for Paris or something! Ooh la la!).

After my boyfriend and I split up, I walked into some Dutch woods and began singing one of my favorite songs from the *Christian Science Hymnal* (with words by Rosa M. Turner) to comfort myself. "O dreamer, leave thy dreams for joyful waking, O captive, rise and sing, for thou art free; The Christ is here, all dreams of error breaking, unloosing bonds of all captivity. He comes to bless thee on his wings of healing; To banish pain, and wipe all tears away; He comes anew, to humble hearts revealing/ The mounting footsteps of the upward way," I sang, singing the words to the tune of "Oh Danny Boy." As I hit the high F, a party of two middle-aged couples emerged into the clearing and listened to me sing the rest of the song. They applauded, and in English told me how beautiful my singing was and thanked me for it. I'll always remember their kind words at that time.

Later, back in London and back-packing to the boarding house where I was going to spend the night, I remember a man's face stuck out of the crowd — he had curly-blond hair and bore an uncanny resemblance to Gene Wilder as he appeared in "Willy Wonka." Our eyes made contact and he smiled a smile of pure joy. Having just broken up with my boyfriend in a strange land, thousands of miles away from my family and friends, that joyful, friendly smile meant everything to me at that moment and I carried it with me back to America and through twenty-some years to the present.

***

In my twenties, while visiting a friend who worked at the Grand Canyon, I decided to hike down to the Indian Gardens, which — if I remember correctly — was about half-way to the canyon bottom. The day I decided to do this it was 110 degrees outside and, for some reason I can't fathom now, I was wearing a pair of dark jeans. I broiled, man. When I reached the Indian Gardens I rested in the cool shade of the cottonwoods and contemplated my trip back up the trail. I knew I'd gotten myself in a bit of a fix. I'd be hiking up that trail in the hottest part of the day, wearing dark jeans, and with no sunscreen or wide-brimmed hat to protect myself from the sun. Foolish, foolish girl. I hadn't thought this through before I'd impulsively started down that trail. I was not looking forward to the hike back.

Taking a deep breath, I reluctantly left the soothing sound of the breeze in the cottonwood leaves and started back up the trail. I hadn't gone far when a German man in his forties or fifties caught up with me. Looking back, I think he recognized that I might need help at some point, although he never hinted at this observation. He kept up a friendly stream of chatter and kept by my side. Every so often he would suggest "we" stop and drink some water — I see now he was making an effort to keep me from getting dehydrated. By the time we were nearing the rim of the canyon, we'd passed three or four people who had their arms draped around the shoulders of companions and were being dragged to the top. In my head I was playing the nightly newscast: "Karen Molenaar, the daughter of well-known mountain-climber, Dee Molenaar, died today while attempting to hike up from the Indian Gardens in the Grand Canyon." How embarrassing that would be for everyone!

Once we reached the top, my faithful German companion thanked me for hiking with him and wished me a good day. The man had been my guardian angel, and *he* was thanking me! (I headed for the nearest lemonade stand.)

***

When my husband and I first moved from Seattle to the country, I felt (naively) that we were moving to a safer place. I quickly designed a three mile walk for myself along country roads and commenced to taking a daily constitutional.

One day I read an article in a *Christian Science Sentinel* about a little girl who had almost been abducted on a country road, but something had happened (I can't remember what now) that had scared the abductor away. I kept returning to this article. I couldn't understand why, but I felt there was some message in it for me somewhere.

The next day I was taking my walk when a car came up beside me with its stereo playing so loud the entire auto's body seemed to shake. The car stopped about 20 feet in front of me, and the passenger – a stocky man with a leering smile – got out of the car and began to walk back to me. I quickly ripped off a tiny blackberry vine from a roadside bush and held it in front of me like I thought I was going to defend myself with it. The man seemed to think that was pretty funny and kept coming. Just before he reached me, though, he suddenly turned and ran back to the car, which peeled out.

It was then I saw the truck coming from the other direction. Apparently the truck had scared the two men in the other car. The truck stopped next to me, and the driver – a man with concern written all over his face – asked me if I was alright. Still clutching my blackberry twig in front of me, I nodded my head yes. He asked me if he could give me a lift back to my house. I told him no, that was

KAREN MOLENAAR TERRELL

alright (at this point I was a little leery about getting in any stranger's vehicle), but thanked him for coming when he did. He was another angel in my life.

***

When my children were still toddlers I use to take them to this great park where they could run across an open field and have fun on a nice set of playground equipment. I met the nicest moms there.

One of the moms I met was a woman in her early twenties with a two year-old. She confided in me that she'd like to start looking for a job soon, but she had no idea what she could do. I listened to her speak — she was articulate, used descriptive language, had great voice. The teacher in me had to ask, "Have you ever thought of being a writer?"

Her eyes opened wide and her mouth fell open. "That's what I've always wanted to do! How did you know?"

I told her she talked like a writer.

We talked a little more and then it was time to leave. But I've thought about that young woman often, and prayed to know that she would find a job where she could fully use her talents. I like to think she has.

***

God has allowed me to cross paths with so many amazing people in my life. I'm filled with gratitude for all our Father-Mother's children.

COMMUNITY

***

"Thou to whose power our hope we give,
Free us from human strife.
Fed by the love divine we live,
For Love alone is Life;
And life most sweet, as heart to heart
Speaks kindly when we meet and part."
From the Christian Science Hymnal, words by Mary Baker Eddy

***

I once told a friend, "You know, I'm a really kind and loving person when I'm by myself. It's when I get around other people that I'm a witch." She laughed and said she knew exactly what I meant, and the same was true for her.

I love people. I'm a great one for chatting with strangers at the supermarket, in an airport lounge, or in the mountains. The challenge, for me, is in being kind and forgiving to the people that I deal with on a daily basis.

I'm lacking in certain social skills. I never would make it past the first week on any of those "Survivor" shows because I have no idea how to go about strategically building alliances or excluding others from my "team." If "Survivor" was actually about surviving in the wilderness on your outdoor skills and physical abilities I might have a fighting chance. But the social component puts me at a distinct disadvantage.

I'm wary of joining groups and making alliances. It seems to me that when you join a group you are agreeing to obey certain unspoken, unwritten rules. You're agreeing to conform to the opinions of the other members of the group. You're agreeing to like and dislike the same people as other members of your group. You're agreeing to have the same world view and politics. You're agreeing to spend time going to events/meetings/parties. I suppose, if being part of the "in" group is a huge priority for a person, then the events/meetings/parties are considered a worthwhile investment of time. But, personally, being the socially lazy person I am and not taking my social duties as seriously as I probably should, I prefer to spend an evening with my family or a few close friends.

It's true that in spite of my social laziness there have been times in my life when I've been rather popular, and it's also true that I find it more fun to be liked than not. But I have to admit that it's when people don't like me so much that I seem to grow the most spiritually. Mary Baker Eddy writes in *Science and Health*, "Human affection is not poured forth vainly, even though it meet no return. Love enriches the nature, enlarging, purifying, and elevating it. The wintry blasts of earth may uproot the flowers of affection, and scatter them to the winds; but this severance of fleshly ties serves to unite thought more closely to God, for Love supports the struggling heart until it ceases to sigh over the world and begins to unfold its wings for heaven."

Mostly, I go through life happily and obliviously bungling my way from one social faux pas to the next, assuming that we're all on the same team, until someone tells me differently.

Thankfully, I have several things going for me on those occasions when I discover that I'm not a part of The Team. Firstly, I have a wonderful and supportive spouse who can always help put my issues with other people in perspective for me. Secondly, I have a wonderful relationship with myself (I crack myself up!). And thirdly — but most importantly — I have a wonderful relationship with my Father-Mother, God. He has been my faithful and best companion through the years, and I know He's always with me, loving and caring for me.

***

Some time ago I had the opportunity to express God's love to my fellow staff members at the school in which I taught in a tangible and, for me, very satisfying way. From what I could gather, a small group of staff members in my school were taking it upon themselves to routinely go to the principal to complain about other staff members. My perception was that many of my co-workers were feeling demoralized, unappreciated, and unloved. There seemed to be a climate of fear in the building. I prayed to find a solution to this problem.

One day as I was taking my daily lunch walk it came to me in a flash what I needed to do for my co-workers.

Many teachers, myself included, have their students write their name at the top of a page, and then pass those pages around the room. As each student gets another student's paper, he writes down something he likes about that person. The list gets passed around the entire room and every student ends up with a "Nice List" for himself. The response to this is always positive. The students are always amazed to learn how much they are loved, and some of the students keep those lists forever.

Well, I decided to do the same kind of thing for the staff at my school. I was very nervous about putting this idea out there – would everyone scoff? Laugh? Refuse to participate? But, I felt this idea was inspiration from God, and knew I had to pursue it. So I sent out an e-mail to the staff, detailing my plan. The response was positive (only two people on the staff of forty asked to be left off the Nice Lists) and so I handed out lists with all the staff members' names on them (except the two who didn't want to participate) and waited to see what would happen.

I am still amazed by the beauty of the words I read from my peers! I discovered a wealth of love in my school. My co-workers were very eloquent in sharing their appreciation for one another, eager to pat each other on the back, articulate in their praise. As I compiled the praise into Nice Lists for each staff member, there were times when I found myself tearing up with gratitude for my co-workers as I read what they had written about each other.

It was Christmastime when I put these lists together, so I printed them out on paper with a Christmas border, laminated them, and handed them out to each of my co-workers as a Christmas gift.

Oh my goodness! Half a dozen people hugged me when they got their lists, another half a dozen thanked me in the halls, and a dozen people e-mailed me to thank me for this gift. My principal e-mailed me, with a "cc" to the rest of the staff, telling me that I had "done a good thing."

Today you'll still find these lists tacked on teachers' walls around the school.

***

Of course, the Nice Lists didn't solve all the conflicts in our school and at the beginning of the next school year the same staffers who had gotten in the habit of going to the principal to criticize others were back at it again.

Once again I went on a solitary lunch walk and prayed about the situation, and, again, an answer came to me. I went back and wrote the following e-mail to my principal, with a "cc" to the rest of the staff:

***

Dave,

In the past I've never come to you with criticism of my peers, always feeling I had enough to do trying to keep myself on task. But this year I've decided to turn a new leaf, as it were, and let you know some of the issues I really think you need to address. Here are a few examples:

1) Hank keeps us laughing much too much in the staff room. There isn't a proper sense of decorum in there. I really think you need to talk with him about this.

2) The 7th/8th grade wing is much too quiet during lunchtime this year. I believe Connie is probably mostly to blame for this. Could you get on her about this?

3) Our new kindergarten teacher has already learned to master double-siding on the copier and is making the rest of us look bad. Please ask her to pretend she has problems with the copier occasionally.

Well, this is a start. I'll send you more criticisms as the year goes on, feeling that you should be kept abreast of this type of thing.

Karen Terrell

***

As with the Nice Lists, the response was amazing! Hank told

me my comments were "scathing," the principal told me my letter was a "classic," and several teachers asked to be the next victims of my "criticisms."

***

My love for music has provided me with a wonderful musical community.

Several years ago I was belting out a hymn at a memorial service with much gusto and fervor and was overheard (well, it would have been hard to "underhear" me at the volume at which I was singing) by this wonderful spiritually-centered Lutheran woman named Julie. Afterwards Julie approached me and asked if I'd be interested in joining her "marymusic" group, whose mission was to visit home-bound people and soothe them to sleep with Christian songs. This sounded right up my alley and I immediately answered in the affirmative.

As part of marymusic, I had some incredibly inspiring experiences.

The last time I sang with marymusic we visited a former co-worker of mine who was battling cancer. I think Kai knew when we visited her that she was dying. (If I were writing here for other Christian Scientists I wouldn't put it in those terms. Instead I'd say something like, "Kai was working on a belief of cancer. The belief was that the cancer was fatal.") But she was the same smartass Kai — and I mean "smartass" in the best sense of the word: Feisty, scrappy, back-talking. Above all, Kai was brimming over with love and emotional strength. She exuded no sense of fear, just an incredible love of life.

Kai requested I sing "Somewhere Over the Rainbow" for her, and so, with Ginny, another former co-worker of ours, on the piano, I sang that song with a new sense of what the words might mean to Kai. "Someday I'll wish upon a star, and wake up where the clouds are far behind me. Where troubles melt like lemon drops, away above the chimney tops — that's where you'll find me." I was in tears by the time I finished, wanting so badly for Kai's troubles to melt away for her, and knowing, without a doubt, that someday they would.

After we left, Kai contacted a friend of hers who worked for a

Seattle newspaper, and her friend ended up doing a piece on Julie's "marymusic." Kai died before the story was published, which brings me to another God-blessing: The morning after Kai died, rocked with grief, I flipped on the radio and guess what song came on? "Somewhere Over the Rainbow!" I just knew that God was telling me Kai had made it over the rainbow, and that I didn't need to cry for losing her. I knew she was fine.

I've always believed in the power of music to soothe and heal. Visiting people who are unable to leave their homes, and singing for them, is, I think, the best possible way for me to use my gift of song. The marymusic singers were told many times how much our music meant to those people we visited, and to their families. Being part of Julie's ministry was a precious gift for me, and I shall always feel blest to have been included by that merry little band of Lutherans.

***

For several years now I've invited people to join me for carol-singing through my neighborhood. The people who come to my gathering are always the "funnest" kind of people — uninhibited, unselfconscious, and ready for a wholesome good time. We usually sing for a half hour or so around the piano, getting our voices tuned up, and then we hit the streets. Last Christmas my next door neighbors greeted us at the door and said, "We've been waiting for you guys!" Then the man of the house shared how some people at his work were lamenting the fact that no one ever goes caroling anymore, and he told them, "Well, they do in Bow!"

When we're done singing to my neighbors about the Lord's birth, we come back to the house for cocoa and cookies, and more singing around the piano. I love the harmonies we come up with, hearing voices blend so perfectly together that they buzz against each other.

Mary Baker Eddy writes in *Science and Health*, "Mental melodies and strains of sweetest music supersede conscious sound. Music is the rhythm of head and heart." I couldn't agree more.

***

BLESSINGS:

About once a month I visit my favorite hairdresser, Judy, for her expert and artistic handling of my hair. Judy is a tough little redheaded fire-cracker from North Carolina, with a raspy twang and a wonderful take on life. She is a steady and consistent part of my community and I look forward to my visits with her.

Judy and I found out early on that we were on the "same team" politically, and so much of our conversations have revolved around what's going on in our country and in the world. We are convinced that if someone would just have the good sense to make us co-Presidents of the U.S. of A., everyone would probably be a lot better off for it.

The first time I saw Judy after 9-11 was about a week after the attacks. We were both unusually quiet, I remember. Neither one of us spoke beyond the normal greetings at first. Finally our eyes met in the mirror. I'd never before seen Judy's eyes with that expression in them. She looked heartsick. "How are you?" I asked her, quietly.

She shook her head in the negative.

"Me, neither," I told her.

We talked a little then, about what had happened, and gave each other a tight hug before I left.

Gradually, as the months passed, we were able to laugh again with each other.

Judy is more than just my "hair lady." She is my friend. She knows a lot of my secrets, and I know many of hers. On the outside we would appear to be very different people — she's a sassy, tobacco-smoking party animal; I'm a church-going schoolteacher. But in the ways that count, I like to think I am very much like her. She has great compassion for the humble. She has no patience with hypocrisy. She prays for peace in the world. She knows how to cut through political b.s. and get to the heart of a matter.

I count myself blest to have Judy in my community.

***

When the United States invaded Iraq two years ago, I felt the need to gather a group of spiritually-minded people together to pray for the world. I sent out word through the e-mail and grapevine that I would have a sharing-of-good-thoughts gathering at my house on Friday at 7:00.

When the clock struck 7:00 on that Friday night, no one had arrived. But I'd made a commitment to set aside an hour to pray, so I asked my husband and son if they'd pray with me for the world and they joined me in the living room.

As soon as we sat down the doorbell rang. I went to answer it and there were eight people standing on my doorstep, all armed with words of hope and peace, and ready to pray with me.

My son, Andrew, read a piece he'd written about the "best gifts" — not material things, but love, honesty, and all those things you can't see with your eyes. I read passages from the Scriptures and from Mary Baker Eddy's *Science and Health* that spoke of the power of Love: "Human hate has no legitimate mandate and no kingdom. Love is enthroned." Wendy, the school bus driver who's a student of Buddhism, spoke of how we should treat other people with the same dignity and respect with which we would want them to treat us. Peggy, a Methodist woman of intelligence and integrity, talked about the logic of peace and caring for one another. Heidi, a fellow middle school teacher who came with her two young children, talked about the importance of community, of people coming together like this to share and create bonds of friendship. Russ, of the Catholic faith, read writings by the Pope which spoke of our duty to work for peace. Carmen, also Catholic, read that wonderful poem by Emily Dickenson entitled "Hope":

***

Hope is the thing with feathers —
That perches in the soul —
And sings the tune without the words —
And never stops — at all —

***

BLESSINGS:

We ended our meeting holding hands and sharing in a moment of silent prayer. It was powerful and profound, that silence.

***

There is a movement of good at work in our world, and we all have an incredible opportunity to be part of this movement. As Mary Baker Eddy wrote in *Science and Health*, "Know thyself, and God will supply the wisdom and the occasion for a victory over evil." I thank God for every occasion we have to prove His goodness and love. I thank Him, too, for the sense of community we find when we gather with like-minded people to work for the cause of Love. That's one investment of time that I'm willing to make.

You, dear reader, are now a part of my community, too.

God bless you richly with infinite blessings!